AFFIRMING GOODNESS

Rev. J. Ronald Knott

Sophronismos Press
Louisville, Kentucky

AFFIRMING GOODNESS

For information address:
Sophronismos Press
1271 Parkway Gardens Court #106
Louisville, Kentucky 40217

Editors: Lori Massey, Marnie McAllister, Tim Schoenbachler
Cover Design & Book Layout: Tim Schoenbachler

First Printing: November 2013

ISBN: 978-0-9858001-4-7

Also by J. Ronald Knott

For more information about eBook and printed editions of all of
Father Knott's books, go to: www.ronknottbooks.com

BOOKS FOR CLERGY

Diocesan Priests in the Archdiocese of Louisville;
Archdiocese of Louisville Vocation Office, 2001

Religious Communities in the Archdiocese of Louisville;
Archdiocese of Louisville Vocation Office, 2002

Intentional Presbyterates:
Claiming Our Common Sense of Purpose as Diocesan Priests;
(Spanish and Swahili editions available) Sophronismos Press, 2003

From Seminarian to Diocesan Priest:
Managing a Successful Transition;
(Spanish edition available) Sophronismos Press, 2004

The Spiritual Leadership of a Parish Priest:
On Being Good and Good At It;
(Spanish edition available) Sophronismos Press, 2007

Intentional Presbyterates: The Workbook;
Sophronismos Press, 2007

A Bishop and His Priests Together:
Resources for Building More Intentional Presbyterates;
Sophronismos Press, 2011

HOMILIES / SPIRITUALITY

An Encouraging Word: *Renewed Hearts, Renewed Church;*
Sophronismos Press, 1995

One Heart at a Time:
Renewing the Church in the New Millennium;
Sophronismos Press, 1999

Sunday Nights: *Encouraging Words for Young Adults;*
Sophronismos Press, 2000

FOR THE RECORD BOOK SERIES

FOR THE RECORD:
Encouraging Words for Ordinary Catholics, Volumes I - XI;
Sophronismos Press 2003 - 2013

To all those on the outer edges of the Church - the mad, the sad, the ignored and the bored - in gratitude for all you have taught me over the last 44 years. It appears you have a new champion in Pope Francis.

Acknowledgments

I would like to thank Mr. Joseph Duerr, former editor of The Record, our archdiocesan newspaper, who originally gave me the opportunity to write these weekly columns. I also thank Mr. Glenn Rutherford for giving me valuable advice along the way. A special thanks to Lori Massey and Marnie McAllister, who edited these columns when they first appeared in *An Encouraging Word*.

I would also like to thank, in a very special way, Mr. Tim Schoenbachler, who has edited and formatted this book and made all of my books, printed new editions and eBooks, available in one convenient place:ronknottbooks.com.

Last of all, I would like to thank the many supportive readers who have encouraged me to keep on writing and who have taken the time to let me know how much these words of encouragement have meant to them.

Table of Contents

INTRODUCTION

Encourage one another.
2 CORINTHIANS 13:11

When I started writing my weekly column, An Encouraging Word, in September of 2002, I did so for two reasons. I wanted to encourage ordinary Catholics not to lose hope during the dark days of the sexual abuse scandal that rocked the Church and I wanted to be of help to the many individuals who have asked me if I could be their personal spiritual director. No longer pastor of a parish, I did not have a regular pulpit nor did I have the time to be a spiritual director to so many individuals. It came to me one day that I could actually have a bigger pulpit and provide spiritual direction if I had a weekly column in our diocesan paper where I could "preach" the over-arching themes of my ministry: affirming goodness, forgiveness and the unbounded measure of God's love.

I could not have imagined that I would still be writing, but I am. I am now well into my twelfth year. I could not have imagined that interest in this column would go beyond the "ordinary Catholics" to whom it was first directed, to people who claim to be "spiritual, but not religious," people of other Christian denominations and religions, as well as people of no particular faith.

It is with those in mind that I have decided to pick out some of the most popular and universal messages of the last eleven years and put them into a book of their own in hopes of reaching even more people who are hungry for spiritual reading.* I have also included a collection of almost 200 memorable and thought provoking quotes cited in those articles of the past eleven years.

Spiritual reading is the practice of reading books and articles about spirituality with the purpose of growing in holiness. It is my hope that these columns might be classified by some as "spiritual reading."

Many of the great saints of the Church recommended "spiritual reading." St. Jerome said that "When we pray we speak to God; but when we read, God speaks to us." St. Ambrose said much the same when he said, "We address him when we pray; we hear him when we read." St. Alphonsus Ligouri said, "Apply to the reading of holy books, not in a passing way and for a short time, but regularly and for a considerable time."

St. Pius X said this about the practice of spiritual reading. "Everyone knows the great influence that is exerted by the voice of a friend who gives candid advice, assists by his counsel, corrects, encourages and leads one away from error. Blessed is the man who has found a true friend: he that has found him has found a treasure. We should, then, count pious books among our true friends. They solemnly remind us of our duties and of the prescriptions of legitimate discipline; they arouse the heavenly voices that were stifled in our souls; they rid our resolutions of listlessness; they disturb our deceitful complacency; they show the true nature of less worthy affections to which we have sought to close our eyes; they bring to light the many dangers which beset the path of the imprudent."

For those wanting to access the original series of *For The Record: An Encouraging Word* books, Volumes I-XI are available at ronknottbooks.com.

Rev. J. Ronald Knott

Many of the original titles of the articles included in this collection have been renamed.

Transitions

The Lord said to Abram, "Go forth from the land of your kinsfolk to a land I will show you." Abram was seventy-five years old when he left Haran. – GENESIS 12:1,4

It's June, a time for major planned transitions of all sorts: graduations, retirements, marriages and ordinations. This does not count unplanned transitions such as deaths, losses of jobs and major health crises. To all my readers going through any major transition, whether chosen or imposed, I would like to offer you an encouraging word.

Anyone confronted by change knows that it is usually followed by a period of emotional upheaval. Unwanted, as well as the most longed for changes have their melancholy, Anatole France points out, because we leave part of ourselves behind and we must die to one life before we can enter another.

Marilyn Ferguson puts it this way: "It's like being between trapezes. It's like Linus when his blanket is in the dryer. There's nothing to hang onto."

All transitions, welcomed and unwelcomed, seem to follow a predictable pattern. There is an entry event, followed by a period of exploration and finally a point of integration.

The entry event could be anything that shakes up our present world to the foundation. It doesn't make much difference whether that event is self-initiated, circumstantial or forced upon us. It is our attitude toward the experience that counts. If we embrace the experience, growth is possible. If we reject the experience, a little more of us withers away.

There are numerous ways to respond to these entry events. We can respond with the curiosity of children and see where they will take us or we can try to run away from them. Somewhere at each entry point, we are faced with a decision. If we say "yes" we have some hope of new life. If we say "no" we remain stuck in anger and depression.

When we say "yes" we enter an exploration phase. We set out warily or enthusiastically. No longer resisting, our minds open up to receive something new. With this new openness, the adventure of transformation can begin.

The initial taste can be so scary that we back out and return to the familiarity of the known, no matter how bad it was. It can also be so empowering that we enter a period of busy-seeking and obnoxious certainty as we try to keep duplicating the initial, powerful experience.

If we don't burn out or drive others crazy during this phase, we are ready to go deeper and move into a comfortable new way of living, a phase of integration, being our new selves, comfortable in our own skin once again.

The transitions necessary for transformation are scary, but what option do we have other than decay and decline, anger and resentment? When we are through changing, we are through! In the words of Dietrich Bonhoeffer, "Faint not nor fear, but go out to the storm and action … freedom, exultant, will welcome your spirit with joy."

June 20, 2013

Second Chances

Sir, give it another year. I will cultivate the ground round it and fertilize it: it may bear fruit in the future. If not, you can cut it down. – LUKE 13

This parable is very personal to me. I cannot read it without my mind going back to 1959 and the first semester, second year of high school seminary.

I came to Louisville from Meade County to attend the former St. Thomas Seminary on Old Brownsboro Road. It was a major adjustment for this little 14-year-old country boy. I was a fish out of water.

Instead of offering counseling, the rector of the seminary called me into his office one day. His exact words to me were, "Mr. Knott! We are sending you home in the morning because you are a hopeless case."

With no one to come to my defense, I had to come to my own defense. I cried for another chance, using words very similar to the words of today's parable. "Father, give me another chance. I will try harder. Then, if things aren't better, you can kick me out."

It worked, and here I stand 45 years later, a priest, because of that "second chance." I came very, very close to giving up that day, but by the grace of God I didn't.

In this amazing parable, Jesus teaches his followers that, since the beginning, God has reached out to his people over and over again. Jesus is the culmination of this long history of opportunities. The God of limitless mercy and compassion is patient with us, hoping that we will "bear fruit" before it is too late, patiently awaiting a response from us until we take our last breath.

Lately, I have never before heard of so many people on the verge of giving up: Catholics on their church, priests on the priesthood, parents on their children, spouses on their marriages and the sick on their treatment. This parable offers a most hopeful message to all of these people.

There is an old story, a favorite of mine, that brings this teaching home. It's about an engineer who designed a tunnel between Switzerland and Austria several years back. He got the idea that the best way to approach the project was to have diggers work from both directions at the same time and meet in the middle.

It was risky, but a much faster method, one that would save lots of time and money. When the day arrived when the diggers were supposed to meet, they didn't. Presuming that he had made a gigantic mistake, he committed suicide. The day of his funeral, the diggers broke through, meeting perfectly. The poor engineer gave up one day too soon.

No matter what others think of you, no matter what you think of yourself, remember this: It ain't over 'til it's over. As long as we are alive, there is hope. With God there are as many second chances as we need.

April 22, 2004

Jesus Never Sleeps

A violent squall came up and waves were breaking over the boat. Jesus was asleep on a cushion. – MARK 4

Have you ever been so scared, so panic-stricken, so overwhelmed with terror that you thought you'd die? Sadly, there are people in this world who live, year in and year out, in sheer terror of losing their lives through violence, grinding poverty or disease.

The passengers on the plane that went down in Pennsylvania on 9/11 were forced to leave this world in a heightened, panic-stricken state. Some terrorists even enjoy watching their victims suspended in a state of panic and terror. It must be a human being's worst nightmare to know clearly that he or she is going to die in a few seconds without the means to stop it.

Most people naturally turn to God in such moments. As the old saying goes, "There are no atheists in foxholes!"

Mark describes such a situation in today's Gospel. Every detail of the story is important. It was evening when they got into a small fishing boat to set sail across open water. A violent squall came up, and waves starting breaking over the boat, causing it to start sinking. Jesus was sleeping. They woke him, and he quieted the seas and their panicked hearts.

Imagine being in a sinking boat, on a lake, in a storm, after dark. Fear of drowning is terrifying. I know. When I was a teenager,

I watched one of my closest friends drown. To this day, I can still see the panic in his eyes as he went down a final time.

Mark's story was, no doubt, based on an actual event, but the fact that it happened is not as important as why the early church put it into its Scriptures. The early church, persecuted for its faith, saw itself besieged by storms, while the resurrected and ascended Jesus seemed to be indifferent and absent from their problems. But they also knew that when they turned to him in prayer and trust, he was able to calm their fear and restore their peace.

Some of you may be going through a rough time right now, feeling that you are sinking or drowning in your problems: a terrible diagnosis, an abusive relationship, a marriage gone bad, a drug-addicted child, an alcoholic spouse, dependent and sick elderly parents, the loss of a job or even bankruptcy. I am sure that some of you have had the feeling that God seems to be absent or asleep or disinterested in your situation.

Today's Gospel holds a message for you – the message that Jesus never sleeps and, when called on, can calm your terrified and worried heart and, in time, make your storms subside.

A 98-year-old friend of mine may have put it best when she said, "I'm not scared of dying. God has always taken care of me, and I trust that when the time comes, he will be there for me again."

August 3, 2006

Self-Pity

Give thanks to the Lord for he is good!
PSALM 118:1

We Christians have preserved, untranslated, the Hebrew word *halleluya* in our liturgies, especially during the Easter season, even from the beginning. *Halleluya* is an expression of thanksgiving, joy and triumph. *Halleluya* means "praise Jehovah God."

I know that I have a lot to be thankful for, but sometimes I let the small aggravations of life take on too much importance. Instead of singing halleluya in response to my many blessings, I catch myself whining about the small stuff. As a reminder, I have a "no whining" symbol taped to my bathroom mirror.

I almost ripped it off the mirror in January and flushed it down the toilet. My new, six-month-old computer crashed. Neither love nor money seemed to help in getting it fixed and back in use, no matter where I took it. Even the "Geek Squad" let me down several times.

During this time, I experienced what I called "a sinus infection from hell" that went on for four weeks. At my sickest point, I lost power for almost a week and had to try to nurse myself back to health in a freezing house with no way to heat my cans of Campbell's chicken noodle soup. During all this, my retirement fund was evaporating by the day.

During one of my worst "whining" episodes, I caught myself and tried to remind myself that even though I was inconvenienced, I did not have a "problem" compared to what many people go through every day of their lives.

Have you ever thought about how much you have to be thankful for, even in this economic downturn? Let's look at some of the things most of us don't even think about.

I have a whole body that works. Many of our courageous Iraqi veterans can't say that. I can eat food through my mouth and digest it. (The next time you complain about "the same old thing for dinner" remember those with feeding tubes and those who haven't eaten in days.)

I can talk and make decisions. (Think about those who have no such freedom in many parts of the world.) I can create new things. I can hear. I can help others. I can see. I have people who love me. I can breathe normally. (Nothing like a four-week sinus infection to make you appreciate something as simple as breathing normally.)

Easter, for me, is the "no whining" season, a season to focus on thanksgiving, joy and triumph. Easter does not promise a life without aggravations or even serious problems and setbacks, but it does promise that there is always hope, recovery and a new day on the horizon.

My favorite Easter reading – one that I used at my first Mass – is the "Walk to Emmaus" where the disciples' "downcast eyes" were replaced with "burning hearts" after they realized that their Master was still walking with them even when they were "unaware."

April 16, 2009

Commitment

I say to myself, I will not mention him, I will speak his name no more. But then it becomes like a fire burning in my heart, imprisoned in my bones; I grow weary holding it in; I cannot endure it. – JEREMIAH 20:9

I love stories about great saints who get so fed up with God that they finally "let him have it!" One of my favorites is about St. Theresa of Avila, maybe the greatest female mystic of our church.

She traveled around Spain trying to reform the convents of her order that badly needed renewal. It was her practice to go to the chapel before one of these long and arduous trips to pray for a safe trip. After one such trip, when everything that could go wrong did go wrong, she stormed into the chapel and yelled, "Listen, God, if this is the way you treat your friends, no wonder you have so few."

was called, against his will, to be a prophet. He tried to beg off, telling God he was too young, too inexperienced and totally unable to speak in public.

God would not accept his excuses. His prophetic preaching evoked deadly hostility. He was put in stocks, he was tried for blasphemy and he was imprisoned for desertion. He was even thrown into a well and left to die by his own relatives.

Jeremiah grew not just tired of the abuse, he steamed with frustration. "Listen, God, you sweet-talked me into this job and then you abandoned me. I am a laughing stock. Your message has brought me nothing but ridicule and rejection all day long. I don't even want to mention your name any more. I'm fed up. I'm finished. I'm out of here."

Then comes that famous "but" in his prayer. "I am furious with you on one hand, but then on the other hand your message is like a fire burning in my heart. It is imprisoned in my bones. I can't help myself. I couldn't quit if I wanted to."

Who hasn't wanted to quit – quit his church, quit his marriage, quit his job or quit being a parent?

It is easy to be ordained, fun to go through a first Mass, exciting to get your first parish. But one doesn't really decide to be a priest until he hits one of those darkest moments. It is then that one really chooses priesthood.

It is easy to be married when you are in love, when everything is exciting. But one really makes the decision to be married when the honeymoon is over, when you face a crisis in your marriage. It is then that you either commit or run.

As Jeremiah discovered, you don't answer a call once, but over and over and over again. You don't just say "I do" once, but "I do" again and again, especially in those dark and confusing times.

October 6, 2005

Blessing People

He who waters will be watered.
PROVERBS 11:25

Like many of you, I have a New Year's resolution. I have decided to double-down on a spiritual practice I began in earnest when I started writing this column more than 10 years ago — the spiritual practice of blessing people.

Nothing has brought more blessings into my life than the practice of looking for people to compliment and encourage and then expressing what I have seen in this column. The idea was simple — look for goodness to affirm rather than evil to condemn. Indeed, "He who waters will be watered!"

Jesus put it this way, "Give and gifts will be given to you; a good measure, packed together, shaken down, and overflowing, will be poured into your lap." (Luke 6:38)

Ever since I have adopted this spiritual practice in a serious way, I have also noticed in an ever sharper focused way how many people, consciously or unconsciously, engage in the mean and ultimately self-defeating practice of withholding compliments. There may be even more who stick their heads out a bit and then pull it back in giving praise, which may be even more cowardly. "The meanest, most contemptible kind of praise is that which first speak well of a man and then qualifies it with a "but," according to Henry Ward Beecher.

Why is it so hard for some people to offer a direct, clear and un\conditional compliment? Why does it seem like an "ascetical" practice that goes against our nature? I guess it goes all the way back to Cain and Abel. Cain became "resentful and crestfallen" because God looked with favor on his brother's offering. This sin is alive and well even in clerical circles. Father Andrew Greeley once wrote (probably about the withholding he felt from his fellow priests in Chicago) that "the worst thing a diocesan priest can do is to get good at something."

We have all heard the old saying, "What goes around, comes around." Paul expands on this wisdom when he writes to the Galatians. "A person will reap only what he sows. Let us not grow tired of doing good, for in due time we shall reap our harvest, if we do not give up. So then, while we have the opportunity, let us do good to all, especially to those who belong to the family of the faith." (6:7-10)

If we need to be loved, appreciated, noticed or honored, the best way to get it is to extend love, show appreciation, pay attention to and honor others.

Writing this column, looking for opportunities to bless others, has brought me more blessings than I could ever have imagined. Hardly a day goes by that I do not get a note, an email, a call or a greeting of appreciation in public places by people I have never met. Writing this is, for me, a spiritual practice. By watering others, I have been watered. This year, give what you need.

January 10, 2013

Gratitude

Walk in him, abounding in thanksgiving.
COLOSSIANS 2: 6, 7

Every spring semester for the last four years I have taught a class called "The Transition into Pastoral Ministry" for the graduating deacons who are about to be ordained priests.

We cover many of the practical realities they will face as new priests as they move out of the seminary and into parishes and religious communities all across the country. We like to call what they are moving into "the real world," even though that doesn't say much about the "reality" of life in the seminary.

One of the things I cover is gratitude: the ability to be thankful for all those who taught them, supported them and cared for their needs during their seminary years. Unfortunately, gratitude is not something that can be taken for granted, even for them. They may be thankful, but in their excitement to move on they may forget to express it.

Using a little "cowboy wisdom," I like to remind them that "when you get to where you are going, take care of the horse you rode in on." In other words, when you get to ordination, be sure to thank those who helped you get there – all the way down to the people who cooked your food and cleaned your classrooms. From all reports, I may be getting through to them.

As we celebrate Thanksgiving Day 2008, I thought it might be a good idea to remind myself and my readers that "thanks" have to be "given" to have a real effect. As a quote from Gladys Browyn Stern puts it, "Silent gratitude isn't much good to anyone."

Of course, our gratitude must go first to God, "from whom all blessings flow." I was always amazed, when I was pastor of the Cathedral, at how many people turned out for Thanksgiving Day Mass. Many years the place was filled. I was so amazed that I secretly wanted to tease them by saying, "Hey! Don't you know that this is not a holy day of obligation?" The sheer numbers who came spoke volumes about their need to give thanks and always made me feel proud to be their pastor.

Secondly, we must train ourselves to give thanks to those around us. One of the issues I address at length when I speak to priests around the country is our inability to affirm one another. We all know it is not good to run each other down, but sometimes we need to be reminded that not "bad mouthing" each other is not good enough. We must learn to build each other up. We must learn to "good mouth" each other. Withheld compliments can be damaging as well.

"Every snowflake in an avalanche pleads not guilty." When enough people withhold their gratitude, then whole communities, whole parishes, whole families and whole presbyterates suffer.

Let us remember not only to be thankful, but also to give thanks to God and all those who help us, support us and love us.

November 27, 2008

Giving Thanks

As you received Christ Jesus the Lord, walk in him, rooted in him and built upon him, abounding in thanksgiving.
– COLOSSIANS 2:6,7

It is odd, but sometimes it seems that those who appear most blessed seem to be the least grateful, while those who appear to be least blessed seem to be most grateful.

Why? I suppose one has to know what it is to not have to appreciate what it is to have. It might be that it is in poverty, rather than in riches, that we become most grateful. As the Estonian proverb puts it, "Who does not thank for little will not thank for much."

Horace might have nailed it better when he said, "Only a stomach that rarely feels hungry scorns common things."

Along that line, H.U. Westermayer has this insight about the origins of our national Thanksgiving holiday: "The Pilgrims made seven times more graves than huts. No Americans have been more impoverished than these who, nevertheless, set aside a day of thanksgiving."

Maybe the original spirit of our Thanksgiving holiday can be summed up best in the words of Epictetus: "He is a wise man who does not grieve for the things which he has not, but rejoices for those which he has."

Aldous Huxley reminds us that "most human beings have an almost infinite capacity for taking things for granted."

In a similar vein, G.K. Chesterton said, "When we were children we were grateful for those who filled our stockings at Christmas time. Why are we not then grateful to God for filling our stockings with legs?"

Even though the Thanksgiving holiday comes but once a year, it can be a mighty reminder to live in a constant state of gratitude — an attitude of gratitude, if you will.

Thornton Wilder made this point: "We can only be said to be alive in those moments when our hearts are conscious of our treasures."

Catholics are called to celebrate Thanksgiving every Sunday. We call it "Eucharist." The reason that so many people say they "don't get anything out of going to church," I believe, is because they go to "get something out of it" rather than go to "take something to it."

The word "Eucharist" means "giving thanks." If we don't count our blessings before we get there, we have no idea what to do when we do get there. Maybe a great American Protestant preacher had the best advice for preparing to celebrate the Eucharist when he said, "Let the thankful heart sweep through the day and, as a magnet finds the iron, so it will find, in every hour, some heavenly blessings!"

November 24, 2011

A New Way of Seeing

I came into this world so that those who do not see might see. – JOHN 9:39

Tyler Perry — African-American playwright, actor and screen-writer — produced and starred in a recent number-one box office hit, "Dairy of a Mad Black Woman." Perry attributes his success to what he calls "spiritual progress," especially, making peace with his own father.

In my estimation, he had a profound insight when he said, "I learned that parents do what they know how." He could have refused to let go of his anger and blame, but he said, "My life changed once things changed in me."

I am amazed when I talk to stuck people. I believe that most people who are stuck are basically people who are blinded by their inability to "see in a new way." They whine and cry and wait to be rescued, but they cannot change their minds and look at their situations from a new angle. They can't let go of their old way of thinking and seeing, and so they remain stuck in their blindness.

They are like the monkeys I read about several years ago. To catch monkeys for the zoo, people would cut a hole in a tree, just small enough for a monkey to stick his hand into. Then they fill the hole with peanuts. When the monkeys stick their hands into the hole and grab the peanuts, they cannot pull their hands back out.

Instead of letting go of the peanuts, monkeys howl and cry till someone comes and hauls them off to the zoo. All they would have to do was to let go of the peanuts. People are a lot like that: they cannot let go of the way they see things and so remain trapped in their suffering. They clutch at beliefs that say life ought to be fair, parents ought to be perfect, spouses should not let each other down, those who lead in the church ought to be perfect, things ought to make sense, and people ought to respect you, love you and meet your needs.

Of course, when it turns out that life isn't fair, when parents and churches aren't perfect, when spouses let each other down, when things don't make sense and when people do not meet their needs, they fall apart and remain stuck in their belief that if they just don't like it enough, it will go away. All they would have to do to free themselves is to let go of their old assumptions and see things in a new way.

Jesus was right when he called for a "metanoia," a new way of seeing and a new way of thinking. Tyler Perry was right on target when he said, "My life changed once things changed in me." When we refuse to change the way we look at things, when things within us resist change, we actually contribute to perpetuating our own suffering.

April 7, 2005

The Choices We Make

Decide today whom you will serve. As for me and my household, we will serve the Lord. – JOSHUA 24:15

It is hard to accept sometimes, but I believe we either choose to be the kind of men and women we end up becoming, or we become the kind of men and women we end up becoming because we fail to choose.

If we choose a life of commitment to doing the right thing, we become men and women of character. If we always choose the easy way and indulge our appetites without self-control or personal boundaries, our lives become burdened with an inward sense of shame, and we will ultimately forfeit self-respect as well as the respect of others.

If we try to split the difference, as many do, we end up in a purgatory of mediocrity and live lives of quiet (or sometimes not so quiet) desperation. Even a failure to choose is a choice that dooms some of us to a hell of regret, when we realize over and over again "the things that might have been."

Blaming others for who we are has been honed to a fine art these days. If we dislike who we are, we have been taught to blame our parents, our upbringing or our circumstances. Maybe we were powerless as children; maybe we were victims of circumstance earlier in life — but most of us are free to live differently in adulthood. George Bernard Shaw says, "This is the true joy in life … the being a force of nature instead of a feverish, selfish little clod of ailments and grievances, complaining that the world will not devote itself to making you happy."

It is hard to live intentionally in today's cultural context, but it is by no means impossible. The ability to say "no" gives us great power. We are free to decide the extent to which we will allow the culture to affect us. We have the power to choose what is good and reject what is bad.

Faced with an opportunity to choose a different way of living, many of us avoid making the choice. We are afraid of having to let go of some favorite old habit, afraid of what people might think of us, afraid of losing control, afraid of having to revise our maps of reality, afraid of all the work that real change will require.

As much as we like to complain, we often really don't want things in our lives to be all that different from the way they are. We both fear and crave becoming different from what we are now. When we choose the comfort of the familiar over the uncertainty of change, or worse, when we do not choose at all, we actually choose to commit personal and spiritual suicide.

The hardest truth of all just might be the knowledge that we have freely chosen to be what we have become, either by making good or bad choices or by failing to choose altogether.

December 9, 2010

Dying and Rising

Unless a grain of wheat falls to the ground and dies, it remains just a grain of wheat, but if it dies, it produces much fruit. – JOHN 12

I have one single grain of wheat in a small vial on my desk to remind me of the message of Easter. I could preserve this grain in this airtight container for years and years and keep it indefinitely. On the other hand, I could plant this single grain of wheat, and, given enough time, I could literally feed the world.

If I were to bury this one single grain in the earth, in a few weeks it would give itself to become a sprout, then a shoot, then a stalk and finally 50 or more new grains of wheat.

Those 50 or more grains, buried in the ground, would soon become 2,500 or more grains.

Those 2,500 or more grains, buried in the ground, would in turn become 125,000 or more grains.

Each time I would do that, the number of grains would expand at a faster and faster rate, even if some were lost to animals, disease or weather. In time, this single grain of wheat could theoretically produce enough wheat to feed the whole world!

Jesus was simply using the image of a grain of wheat, giving its life to produce millions more grains of wheat, to talk about his own death and resurrection. A grain of wheat is ineffective and unfruitful as long as it is preserved in safety and security, and it only bears fruit when it is thrown into the cold ground and buried, as in a tomb. So it was with the death of Jesus.

His death on the cross and burial in the earth would lead to his resurrection and new life for millions upon millions of his followers – indeed, for all humankind.

This did not just happen once with the historic death and resurrection of Jesus. This is a basic life principle. "Whoever tries to save his life will lose it, and whoever loses his life for my sake will save it." "Life coming through death" is life's biggest paradox.

This process can be accepted or initiated. Often life brings us unexpected or unwanted changes, changes that take us into new places, welcomed or not. Sometimes we get up the courage to initiate a crisis to set the process in motion: we leave crippling relationships, sign ourselves into a treatment and quit jobs that are killing us.

In a way, we "bury" our old life in the belief that it is the path to a new one. The secret is to embrace the dying and rising process, trusting that it will bring us the new life we need and want.

If we live this mystery – dying and rising over and over again – when we get to the end of our earthly lives, we can even embrace our own death, knowing that this life will simply be traded in for a life that we cannot begin to imagine.

May 4, 2006

The Path to Christ

You are Peter and upon this rock I will build my church and the gates of hell shall not prevail against it. – MATTHEW 16

Are you saved? Have you been born again? Have you accepted Jesus as your Lord and Savior? If you really want to make a Catholic squirm and doubt their religious upbringing, just corner one and rattle off that set of questions.

When I worked in the Bible Belt, down in the southern part of the state, Catholics, including myself, were often bombarded with those questions. More than one Catholic was left confused and bewildered. Their counterparts could date the precise hour they were saved, while Catholics stood there puzzled and confused.

Does one have to have a dramatic, certain and dated experience, or can one grow toward God in an extended process, sometimes without a clear beginning or end? In Saints Peter and Paul we see both types of conversion experiences: Paul with his definite and certain experience of conversion at a particular moment and Peter with his long and extended process of conversion over time.

Many of our fundamentalist brothers and sisters look to the Apostle Paul as their hero and ideal. His conversion was a shattering, clearly memorable confrontation with the person of Christ on the road to Damascus when he was on his way to hunt down Christians and kill them. After this dramatic about-face, Paul fanatically embraced what he had recently persecuted and attacked. His conversion experience was so dramatic that the story is retold three times in the Acts of the Apostles and referred to three more times in various New Testament letters.

Paul's emphasis on personal and individual faith, his emphasis on dramatic decision and evangelistic zeal have become the prototype and model of conversion for some Christian groups, especially for fundamentalist groups. Many of these attach a certain spiritual superiority to this type of conversion, leaving many people who have not has such an experience feeling inferior and second rate.

Roman Catholics, while respecting Paul's experience, look to the Apostle Peter as their hero and model. Peter's experience was very different. Peter does in fact make his profession of faith, but, like many of us, it is the climax of a long and gradual insight into who Jesus was.

Even though some would like to suggest that everybody has to have a definite conversion experience that can be dated, the New Testament does not suggest a single stereotype for an authentic Christian conversion experience. The fact is, the church has always welcomed both kinds of experiences. God calls us in a variety of ways. If you have never been "knocked off your horse," you need not feel inferior or apologetic. We all answer God's call in our own way and in the way we are called, be it like Paul or Peter.

With all that said, the fact remains that all of us, sooner or later, must choose or reject Jesus and the path he invites us to walk.

July 24, 2003

Quieting the Noise

When Jesus heard that John the Baptist had been killed,
he withdrew in a boat to a deserted place by himself.

– MATTHEW 14:13

As many times as I have read these lines, I never really paid much attention to them. For some reason, they jumped out and grabbed my attention recently. What Jesus did in response to John's murder is exactly what I do when I face loss, tragedy or illness. I know that I am in a minority, but I want to be left alone. Some people draw their strength from being with people at such times. I get my strength from being away from them. My way is not better than the other way; it is just different.

I believe Jesus was an introvert who was able to balance his need to be alone with his desire to be with people. There are so many stories of Jesus accepting invitations to dinner parties that it earned him the nicknames of glutton and drunkard.

On the other hand, he started his ministry with a forty-day desert retreat, alone. He often took his disciples away to quiet spots when the crush of people got to be too much. Sometimes he retreated to a garden or a mountain or a desert and sometimes in a boat anchored out on a lake. Hours before he died, we find him praying alone in the garden of Gethsemani. Jesus embraced the world, but he got his strength, insight and guidance by withdrawing to the quiet.

The best place to hear God's guiding voice may be in the quiet, but finding that time was a problem for Jesus, as it is for us. Sometimes there was so much coming and going that Jesus and his disciples didn't even have time to eat.

We know that sometimes he got up earlier than others so as to have some quiet time alone. Sometimes he sent his disciples on ahead so that he could enjoy a quiet walk by himself. If he were here today, he might turn off his car radio on the way to work. He might rise early and take his coffee out on the deck. He might jog, rent a cabin or retreat to a local monastery for a day. Where there is a will, there is a way.

The noisier the world gets, the further away from God it gets. As Jeremiah learned, it is not in the noise of winds, earthquakes or fires that we hear God speak to us. It is in that small, whispering voice that can be heard only in the quiet. I have learned one thing from years of counseling: Most people already know the solution to their problems. I don't need to give advice nearly as much as I need to encourage them to shut out the noise and listen to the wisdom of their own hearts. It is there that God speaks, offering direction and strength. In a noisy world, find some quiet, no matter how busy you are.

November 7, 2002

The Perfect Prayer

God answered Solomon's prayer in these words, "Because you have asked for this - not for a long life for yourself, nor for riches, nor for the life of your enemies, but for under-standing so that you may know what is right - I do as you requested." – 1 KINGS

I own a lot of books. I rarely open most of them, but every once in a while I go digging through them looking for some-thing I remember reading a long time ago. There are, however, a few books that I would really hate to lose, books that have changed my life in one way or another. One of those books is an old book by Louis Evely entitled *Our Prayer*.

The insight I got from that book changed my prayer life and helped me make sense of the purpose of prayer. My prayer until then had been very much like that old farmer in one of my former parishes who said that he never prayed for rain because "God's gonna do what God's gonna do anyway!" That old book helped me discover that, even though I believed in prayer, I was actually praying like a pagan!

How do pagans pray? They whine, beg, cringe and bribe their moody, mean and reluctant gods to loosen up and give them what they want. Their prayers are attempts to get their gods to wake up and pay attention! Pagan prayer has been por-trayed best in those old TV jungle movies. Inevitably, a tribe of natives lived at the foot of an active volcano where their god lived. Their volcano god was moody and unpredictable and often blew his top, killing hundreds of tribesmen. To humor their god, they offered bribes as a way to keep him at bay and to do their bidding. Their sadistic god seemed to be especially impressed by pain, so if they drew blood they seemed to have a better chance of getting a favor out of him. If that didn't work, they threw the prettiest virgin in town into the bubbling lava! Pagan prayer was always an effort to get their god to change: change his mind, his sadistic behaviors or his indifference toward human beings.

One of my favorite scriptures about prayer is the story of the wise King Solomon. God "appeared to Solomon in a dream one night, inviting him to ask for something in prayer." Solomon, young and inexperienced as a king, asks simply for what he needed to be a good king: an "understanding heart" and "the wisdom to know right from wrong." He could have asked for selfish needs: a long life, riches or vengeance on his enemies! Solomon teaches us the purpose of all prayer: to have God change us, rather than having us change God, as pagans try to do to their gods. The perfect prayer, as Solomon knew, is to know our calls and to ask only for the "daily bread" we need to live them out.

March 6, 2003

Finding Time to Pray Each Day

Prayer of this kind is good.
1 TIMOTHY 2:3

Most of us who believe in the practice of prayer find it hard these days to find time to pray. Sadly, this is true of many priests as well. Since we cannot create more hours in a day, we have to be clever and imaginative with the hours we have.

My favorite place to pray privately has become my car. It is one of the few places left where I am not interrupted or distracted. Since I drive back and forth from Louisville to Saint Meinrad once or twice a week, I have more time to pray than I first thought.

When I started working at Saint Meinrad a little more than three years ago, I would never think of leaving home without a stack of CDs or tapes or turning on the radio to fill the time in my car. For more than a year now, I have made the trip in total silence. I have grown to love it and look forward to it. In this silence, my mind seems to naturally turn to prayer. The scenery makes it even more conducive to praying.

On Mondays, to miss the downtown morning rush, I usually get up at 4:30 a.m. and, with coffee in hand, I am on the road by 5:15 a.m. Some mornings I can see a beautiful red sun coming up over the horizon, and on occasion a full moon fills my rear view mirror. In the fall, waves and waves of colorful trees blanket the hills. In the winter those same trees, gray and bare, stand quietly in new snow. In the spring, redbuds and dogwoods precede the contagious darkening of green leaves.

Part of the trip takes me through the Hoosier National Forest. From childhood, I have known that "the woods" is a place of wonderment, a sacred space. A little bit of that sacredness seeps into me, even if I am only driving through it.

Racing cars and roaring trucks pass me easily even when I am pushing the speed limit myself. They are made frantic by some unknown pressure, and I pray for their peace of mind.

Laborers in pickups and mothers in minivans all get prayed for as I drive along in silence.

I pass farms where I am reminded, up close and personal, to be grateful for my daily bread — where it comes from and what it takes to get it to me. I pray for these and indeed all farmers.

I usually arrive as thunderous bells gather the monks for their 5:30 a.m. prayer time. As I walk into the huge complex, it is not lost on me that I work at a place saturated with 150 years of such praying.

This is my prayer time. I recommend that you find your prayer time, your special time/place where you can sit in the presence of God in gratitude and bless the people in the world around you.

January 24, 2008

The Purpose of Prayer

Your father already knows what you need before you ask him. – MATTHEW 6:8

I still remember standing in front of church a few years back having a discussion with some farmers about whether to pray for rain. The majority thought it was a good idea. Whatever their personal beliefs about the effectiveness of such prayer, the majority were not about to show any doubt in front of their pastor. One man, however, risking the ridicule of the more pious, stepped up to the plate. "Why pray? God's going to do what God's going to do anyway."

That discussion raised prayer's most fundamental question: "What is the purpose of prayer?" The majority believed that their prayers might influence God to pay attention to their plight and send the rain they wanted. The minority believed that what he wanted didn't matter to God, and he would have to accept whatever God already had in mind to do with his rain.

Both, however, approached the situation with one of the most basic misunderstandings about prayer. The purpose of prayer is not to inform God about our needs nor to influence God to change his mind about meeting our needs. The purpose of prayer, fundamentally, is to get us to change and want what our good God wants to give us.

In this regard, my prayer has changed radically in the last part of my life. I used to pray that I would get assigned to the parish I most wanted, that I would win the lottery or that I would get an "A" on a test. I was usually disappointed in the short run, but in the long run God gave me all I needed and then some. The parish I least wanted turned out to be better. I didn't win the lottery, but I have never been in serious want, either. I didn't always get an "A," but I did graduate with pretty good grades. All in all, I have to admit that if I had gotten all that I asked for, my life would not be as full as it is today.

My prayer now is more about asking God to help me trust him with the things that happen in my life. My prayer now is not about trying to change God or asking him to change my circumstances, but asking God to change me so that I can accept or change my circumstances, knowing that great blessings often lie hidden within circumstances that only appear to be bad at the present time.

When you pray, do you ask God to change and conform to your will, or do you ask God to change you to conform to his will? This change of focus could radically change your prayer life for the better.

December 3, 2009

Unanswered Prayers

If you know how to give good gifts to your children, how much more will the heavenly Father give good things to those who ask him? – MATTHEW 7:11

A few years ago, Garth Brooks came out with a song entitled "Unanswered Prayers." The chorus goes like this: "Sometimes I thank God for unanswered prayers. Remember when you're talkin' to the man upstairs that just because he doesn't answer doesn't mean he don't care. Some of God's greatest gifts are unanswered prayers."

The point of that song is the same as the teaching of Jesus about prayers in the Gospels of Matthew and Luke. In those passages, Jesus tell us that if we "ask, seek and knock" we will "receive, find and the door will be opened," but he also reminds us that our heavenly father, being a good father, will only give us "good things," not merely "things that look good" to us. Jesus uses three powerful examples.

If we ask for bread, he will not hand us a rock even if, from a distance, it looks a whole lot like a brown, round loaf of bread. If we ask for a fish, he will not hand us a dangerous, inedible eel just because it looks a whole lot like a fish. If we ask for an egg, he will not hand us a poisonous scorpion just because it looks whole a lot like a speckled egg when it is curled up in a nest.

God, just like any good parent, would never give one of his children a bottle of poison just because he cries out for it. Just so, what sometimes looks good to us may not be good for us at all. "Some of God's greatest gifts are unanswered prayers."

We have an example of this truth in the well-known incident in the life of Saint Paul when he suffered from a painful affliction he called "a thorn in the flesh," an unnamed physical disability that hounded and limited him. Three times he prayed to have this "thorn" taken away, but the "thorn" was not removed.

Instead, he received the grace of God to endure it and insight into why it was given to him. God seemed to say to him, "What it is doing for you is of far more value than anything that would come from its removal." With that, Paul began to see that, behind his disability, God's good purposes were at work.

December 10, 2009

Untying the "Knots"

With God all things are possible.
MARK 10: 27

Father John Cole of the Archdiocese of Cardiff in Wales started it. After the retreat I gave the priests there last June, he told me that they had decided to call their follow-up program "Untying the Knott." A month later, I got the following prayer in my email box. Actually, these plays on my name do not aggravate me one bit. I was actually honored by the priests of Cardiff, and there is much about this anonymous prayer that I like.

The "Knots Prayer"

Dear God, please untie the knots that are in my mind, my heart and my life. Remove the have nots, the can nots and the do nots that I have in my mind.

Erase the will nots, may nots, might nots that may find a home in my heart. Release me from the could nots, would nots and should nots that obstruct my life.

And most of all, dear God, I ask that you remove from my mind, my heart and my life all of the "am nots" that I have allowed to hold me back, especially the thought that I am not good enough. Amen.

I resonate with the sentiments of this prayer, because they affirm some of my most basic beliefs about life, which can be summarized in a series of what have become some of my favorite quotes. "The biggest human temptation is to settle for too little." (Thomas Merton) "Impossible things just take a little longer." (Philo T. Farnsworth) "Start by doing what is necessary, then what is possible, and suddenly you are doing the impossible." (St. Francis of Assisi) "May you not forget the infinite possibilities that are born of faith." (Mother Teresa)

Why do so many people get bogged down in negative thinking and self-defeating talk. Because it was a normal part of my life as a young man, I have examined this very subject carefully. The answer I finally had to accept was — it is because we are lazy! When we declare a situation hopeless and impossible, we don't have to do anything — we're off the hook! Who would expect a thinking person to waste their time on something that is "hopeless" and "impossible?"

It doesn't take Oprah, Dr. Phil or Maury to realize that low self-esteem lies at the bottom of many of society's problems. These programs follow problems back to childhood, when important adults in their lives were either incapable or unwilling to "parent." Without their critical input, children begin to think that they are useless, life is hopeless and the future is dismal. When these thoughts become part of their way of thinking, many children grow up going down a path of self-destruction and violence toward others that is extremely hard to reverse.

Finally, if you are one of those who missed good parenting, your situation is not hopeless. Do what hundreds of others have done: "parent" yourself no matter how old you are!

January 20, 2011

Attitude Is Everything

Before man are life and death, whichever he chooses shall
be given him. – SIRACH 15:17

Sir Ranulph Fiennes is credited with one of my favorite
quotes: "There is no such thing as bad weather, only inappropriate clothing."

It sums up the tremendous power we have — the power to
choose our response in any given situation. The first time I consciously made this choice and learned this lesson was back in
1970 — the year I was ordained. I had just made my priestly
"promise of obedience" to the bishop two weeks earlier.

When the priest personnel board called to tell me that I was
being sent to Somerset, Kentucky, I panicked. I had my heart
set on a nice cushy suburban parish here in Louisville and the
last place I wanted to go was to the "home missions."

To no avail, I pleaded, begged and cried in an effort to get
them to change their minds. Angrily, I packed my car, bought a
map and headed south. Half way down there, I decided to
change my mind about going. Since I did not get what I
wanted, I consciously decided to want what I got.

To paraphrase Sir Ranulph Fiennes, "There are no bad assignments, only bad attitudes." That choice made the difference between the 10 wonderful years I had and the 10 miserable
ones I could have had.

Over the years, the lesson I learned at the beginning of my
ministry has served me well. It has become a spiritual practice
I have tried to intentionally cultivate over the last 42-and-a-half

years. At the beginning of a new year, this lesson is something I want to remember and share with you. To do so, I have turned to my collection of quotes, my treasure trove of collected wisdom.

"If you don't think every day is a good day, just try missing one." (Cavett Robert)

"A happy person is not a person in a certain set of circumstances, but rather a person with a certain set of attitudes." (Hugh Downs)

"You're not going to make me have a bad day. If there's oxygen on earth and I'm breathing, it's going to be a good day." (Cotton Fitzsimmons)

"If you have nothing to be grateful for, check your pulse." (Unknown)

"The greatest discovery of my generation is that a human being can alter his life by altering his attitudes." (William James)

"I cannot change the direction of the wind, but I can adjust my sails." (Unknown).

"The last of the human freedoms is the ability to choose how we will respond to any given situation." (Viktor Frankl)

Attitude is everything. I remember handing out little cards to the workmen who did the restoration work on our cathedral. It was called "The Bricklayers."

It says, "When three bricklayers were asked what they were doing, the first man answered gruffly "I'm laying bricks." The second man replied with resignation, "I'm putting up a wall." The third man said enthusiastically, "I'm building a cathedral."

January 17, 2013

Our Godlike Power

God created humankind in his own image, in the divine image he created them. – GENESIS 1:27

There is an old story from another religious tradition that I have always found fascinating, a story about the creation and fall of humankind. According to this tradition, humankind was created in the beginning to be like God, but somehow lost its awareness of divinity by turning away from God.

After this loss, the angels got together to decide where to hide the secret of humankind's divinity so that humans would never find it. One angel suggested that they hide it deep in the earth. This idea was rejected, because the other angels feared that humans might one day tunnel deep into the earth and find it.

A second angel suggested that they place it on some distant star. Again the other angels rejected the idea fearing that some-day humans might walk upon the stars and find it.

After considering many ideas, the angels finally decided that they would bury this secret deep within humans them-selves because they knew they would never think to look there. And so they buried the secret of our divinity deep within us, and even today we do not know to look there.

As the book of Genesis tells us, every one of us has been created in the image and likeness of God, with godlike quali-ties and powers within us. However, many of us never realize our true nature, nor act on it. It lies buried within us like some undiscovered treasure.

When we are unaware of our own godlike power, we tend to turn our lives over to others. When we do that, we end up becoming victims of what other people decide for us, all the while complaining of the outcome.

We end up like the rider on a runaway horse in a story I read years ago. A farmer was walking down the road when a man on a bridleless horse galloped by him. The farmer called out, "Hey, where are you going?" The panicked rider yelled back, "Don't ask me, ask the horse!"

When we are unaware of our own godlike power and turn our lives over to others, we often end up blaming and reviling them for our unhappy conditions. We blame our unhappiness and sad situations on dead parents, old teachers, former spouses and even God himself. This is a simple way of excusing our own laziness when faced with the job of building a life for ourselves.

When we are unaware of our own godlike power, we often fall into the trap of conforming, without question, to the values of the popular culture so that others will approve of us. Slaves of conformity, our life script becomes, "Everybody else is doing it."

As Marianne Williamson writes, "Our deepest fear is not that we are inadequate. Our deepest fear is that we are powerful beyond measure. It is our light, not our darkness, that most frightens us."

March 25, 2004

The Path to Holiness

After he had sat down, his disciples came to him and he began to teach them. – MATTHEW 5:1-12

What are the traits of a "holy" person? One who bears a title and wears a robe? Not necessarily.

One who lives isolated in a monastery or hermitage? Maybe. One who is able to quote the Bible, chapter and verse? Sometimes.

What are the traits of a holy person? Jesus tells us, very simply, what holiness looks like. He says that a holy person has several qualities.

Blessed are the poor in spirit. People who are holy are first of all people who put their relationships with God and people above everything else in life. They have their priorities straight.

Blessed are they who mourn. People who are holy are not so jaded and self-centered that they no longer have the ability to feel compassion for those who suffer. Holy people are the opposite of cold and heartless people.

Blessed are the meek. People who are holy know their strengths and weaknesses. They neither inflate their worth nor devalue it. "Holy" people have an unpretentious, down-to-earth goodness about them.

Blessed are they who hunger and thirst for righteousness. People who are holy want to get to know God more, want to become better people and are passionate about trying to do what God asks of them. Knowing God and serving God are the central passions of holy people.

Blessed are the merciful. People who are holy give other people a break, the benefit of the doubt, a good hearing, rather than a rush to judgment. They withhold judgment and extend mercy, knowing that they cannot see into other people's hearts.

Blessed are the clean of heart. People who are holy are people who do the right thing and also do it for the right reason. What you see is what you get. Who they appear to be and who they really are match up perfectly.

Blessed are the peacemakers. People who are holy go out and look for opportunities to heal, to reunite, to bring together and to put an end to strife and misunderstanding. They cannot rest until unity and harmony are restored.

Blessed are they who are persecuted. People who are holy are persecuted. Evil cannot bear the presence of goodness. No good deed, or good person for that matter, goes unpunished. The brighter the light, the fiercer the attack. "Holy" people are often hated, abused, persecuted and even killed, simply because they are good.

Blessed are you when they insult and persecute you because of me. People who are holy are not afraid of being known as a friend of God. They do not shove their religion into others' faces, but neither do they hide it.

This kind of person stands in stark contrast to the money-grubbing, cold-hearted, self-inflated, quick-to-judge, self-centered, opportunistic materialist that the world encourages us to be. Lent calls us to examine our lives and to get back on track. The track we are to get back on is the path of discipleship, the path to holiness.

March 3, 2005

Becoming Saints

Blessed are those who hunger and thirst for righteousness.
MATTHEW 5:6

This week we celebrated the feast of All Saints. All week I found myself humming that old spiritual that goes: "We are all traveling in the footsteps of those who've gone before, but we'll all be reunited on a new and sunlit shore. Oh when the saints go marching in, when the saints go marching in! Oh Lord, I want to be in that number when the saints go marching in!"

I also looked up that old story about Thomas Merton and Robert Lax when he asked Merton what he wanted to be.

"I don't know; I guess what I want to be is a good Catholic," Merton answered. Robert Lax shot back, "What do you mean, you want to be a good Catholic? What you should say is that you want to be a saint!" In defense, Thomas Merton responded, "How do you expect me to become a saint?" "By wanting to," was Lax's response.

With that, Thomas Merton realized the false humility that makes people say they cannot do the things they must do, cannot reach the level that they must reach — the cowardice that says: "I am satisfied to save my soul, to keep out of mortal sin," but means, "I do not want to give up my sins and my attachments."

How many of us really want to be saints, "to be in that number when the other saints go marching in?" Most of us are like

Saint Augustine when he prayed, "Lord, make me pure, but not yet!" Most of us wouldn't mind being a saint if we didn't have to change anything, especially making the change of letting go of our sins and attachments.

Saints are not "perfect people." Saints are people who hunger and thirst for righteousness, people with a drive for improvement — both in who they are and what they do. It's people with a fierce commitment to their own lifelong formation, an unflinching quest for personal excellence.

This does not mean we earn our way to sainthood through personal growth and good deeds. It means that we realize to the depths of our being that we are so loved by God that we want to respond to that love by trying to become all that we can be.

In his book, *The Pursuit of Excellence*, Tom Peters says about himself, "The idea of mediocrity scares the hell out of me!" Maybe that is the secret ingredient in becoming a saint — "the fear of mediocrity," the settling for "good enough to get by with."

We are in truth "saved by grace." We are called to sainthood, and we are given the grace to respond. We do not come to grace; grace comes to us. We cannot will ourselves to grace, but we can open ourselves to its miraculous coming. We can certainly cooperate with God in the process of becoming saints "by wanting to."

November 5, 2009

The Uselessness of Fear

Fear is useless; what is needed is trust.
LUKE 8:50

I've picked up a bad habit since my shoulder surgery last summer. I worry obsessively about my health. Since I have not been seriously sick since the third grade, I really didn't have any idea know how to handle it.

A headache becomes an imagined brain tumor. A toothache becomes an imagined mouth cancer. A rash becomes an imagined outbreak of leprosy.

Even my doctor made fun of me. At the end of the last annual physical, he said, "Well, I didn't find anything, but I can keep looking till I do!" Not funny!

Here is one event out of several that I could tell you about during this past year. Just recently, my dentist told me that he needed to replace a 20-year-old crown with a bridge, which would require an extraction.

Since I have not had a tooth extracted since I was a child, my mind went wild. I imagined I would be housebound for days, condemned to sleepless nights of excruciating pain that large amounts of morphine could not assuage, during which I would curse God, die and go to hell!

After two weeks of enduring an imagination run amok, the day arrived. Like a man on death row, I was ready to get it over with. As I was having my last meal of decaf coffee, the phone rang. It was the dentist's office telling me that the appointment would have to be put off because the power had gone out that morning in New Albany and they could not open. That meant the death sentence had been commuted for five more days, and I was sentenced to another round of worry and dread.

Well, when the day actually arrived, the reality was quite different. I felt no pain during the procedure and very little afterwards. I was a bit disappointed.

OK, maybe I am exaggerating for emphasis, and a lot of this is tongue-in-cheek. However, I have been worrying about things a little more than I used to.

Most people experience short-lived periods of worry without incident. Indeed, a moderate amount of worrying may even have positive effects if it prompts people to take precautions, such as fastening their seat belts or buying fire insurance, or avoid risky behaviors, such as angering dangerous animals or binge drinking.

Normal worry is described as a response to a moderate challenge for which the subject is inadequately prepared. Useless worry, however, is when an undisciplined mind makes you suffer before you have to — what my mother called "crossing your bridges before you get to them."

Thomas Jefferson put it this way: "How much pain they cost us, the evils which have never happened." I have always heard that F-E-A-R stands for "fantasy events appearing real."

Jesus is right: "Fear is useless." One of the best pieces of advice I have come across is this anonymous quote: "For peace of mind, resign as general manager of the universe."

October 20, 2011

Irrational Beliefs

Turn away from me the reproach which I dread.
PSALM 119:39

Not too many weeks ago, I went to the mail box and there found a large envelope containing four letters forwarded to me from The Record office. I opened it and put the four letters down on the table with a twinge of dread. I had this over-whelming fear that at least half of them were going to be complaints from angry people about something that I had written in this column. I argued with myself about opening them or putting it off, but eventually I decided to get it over with!

All of them were very positive, but I spent quite a bit of time trying to analyze my irrational fear of rejection, even though hundreds of people have told me that they like the columns, even love them. Why am I, after all this time, so un-nerved by that poison letter that I get every now and then?

I went to the internet and typed "irrational fears." I was comforted by the fact that I am not necessarily crazy, but my reaction is something that a lot of people go through. Cyclist Lance Armstrong said something that described my experience perfectly. "A boo is louder than a cheer. If you have ten people cheering and one person booing, all you hear is the booing."

Psychologist Albert Ellis identified a number of dysfunctional beliefs that many hold to some degree. Here is a summary.

- It is necessary for me to be loved and approved of by everybody.

- If I am not adequate in all aspects, then I am a worthless person.

- People must be considerate and act fairly at all times, or they are damnable villains if they do not.

- It is awful and terrible if things are not the way I would like them to be.

- My emotional disturbances are always externally, caused, and I have no internal power to exert any control over them.

- If something is, or may be, dangerous or fearsome, I must be constantly and obsessively concerned about it.

- I cannot face life's responsibilities and difficulties, and so I must do everything I can to avoid them.

- I must be dependent on others, because I cannot run my own life.

- Because something affected me adversely in my past life, it must affect me that way today.

- I must feel upset by other people's disturbances, because they feel upset by them.

- There is a right and perfect solution to every human problem, and it is awful when that solution is not found.

One of the four letter-writers gave me some advice about my falling into at least three of these irrational beliefs. "I hope you would not let a few negative people keep you from writing. It is refreshing to know the love you have for sinners like myself!"

September 6, 2012

Cowardly Communication

Wrath and hatred are hateful things.
SIRACH 27:30

After all these years, approximately 20 years to be precise, I still remember it! I was standing at the door of the Cathedral of the Assumption greeting people on their way out. I was in a great mood. The people passing me by were shaking my hand and smiling as they walked by.

Then, out of nowhere, a man got up in my face and hissed, "You ought to be ashamed of yourself!" To this day, I still have no idea what he was talking about. My best guess was it was something I said in the homily.

Those in the world of ministry call it a "drive-by comment." After unloading, the person rushes on, making sure there is no time for question or comment. It belongs in the same category as the "anonymous letter" and the "hit-and-run email."

I don't get them often, but I got an unsigned letter recently with no return address. It was filled with rants that I could not understand, to the point that I am not sure the writer had the right priest. Since I am one of those people who can get 500 compliments and one criticism and find the criticism more believable, these days I destroy unsigned letters immediately lest their destructive poison gets into my system.

The perfect outlet for angry attacks is the internet. I do not get many "hit-and-run emails," but I do know that there is a lot of anonymous viciousness going around in blogs and on social media sites.

The "venial sin" of these cowardly communications is the deliberate withholding of compliments as a way to "get" people. It is more passive-aggressive than a direct hit but can do its own form of damage. "I would have said something, but I didn't want you to get the big head!"

There are many reasons why people turn their frustrations on one another. The pressures produced by uncertainty and confusion are many, and they often produce high degrees of anxiety that people try to manage by primitive processes of scapegoating and projection. We are all susceptible to being victims as well as perpetrators.

If you are a victim, here are a couple of tips. Never read an unsigned letter. Throw it away before it hooks you and upsets your equilibrium. If you are verbally ripped without obvious cause, stop and ask yourself, "What is the problem behind this problem?" Usually you are just the misplaced target for their rage, rather than the real cause.

If you are a perpetrator, one of those people who writes angry letters, sends emails or makes phone calls while drinking or in a foul mood, wait two days before mailing your letter, sending your email or making your call. When you are sober and rested, more often than not, you will decide not to send your blast or make your angry call. If you wait, your communication will no doubt be more civil.

June 28, 2012

Beginning Anew

> Whoever is in Christ is a new creation: the old things have passed away; behold, new things have come. And all this is from God. God was reconciling the world to himself in Christ, not counting their trespasses against them.
>
> – 2 CORINTHIANS 5:17-19

We are in a month named after the Roman god Janus, an appropriate personification of the start of a new year. Janus was pictured with two faces so that he could look ahead toward the future and back at the past, both at the same time.

Like Janus, every year in this month named after him, we look back at the mistakes we have made in the past year, and we look forward to the improvements we hope to make in the coming year.

What is wonderful about a "new" year is the feeling that we can start all over and begin anew. What is wonderful about our faith is that the ability to start over and begin anew is not just a feeling, but a reality.

When we look back over our sins of the past year, we know that, in God, we are forgiven and that we are given a new chance, regardless of what we have done or failed to do.

Realizing that our sins are forgiven and forgotten, we know that we can make a fresh start. We are used to people holding our mistakes against us. They remember our sins and remind us of them, maybe for years. With God, because he forgives and forgets, we can make a new beginning. God does that for us every day, but January 1 is the day we remember it most clearly.

In Scripture, it seems that God is more concerned about our learning from our sins than keeping count of them. He seems to want us to admit our mistakes, not so that we will feel bad about making them, but so that we can make progress in overcoming them.

Devoid of introspection, stupid people keep repeating the same mistakes over and over again — either because they deny them or blame others for them — instead of owning them. Wise people admit their mistakes easily. They know progress accelerates when they do.

Examination of conscience and confession of sins, a basic tradition in the Christian faith, has been misunderstood and even ridiculed by our culture. We hear people cynically refer to "Catholic guilt."

What they are talking about is "Catholic shame." "Guilt" says "I have made a mistake." "Shame" says "I am a mistake." If the church helps us feel "shame" because of who we are, that is bad. If the church helps us feel "guilt" because of the evil we do, that is good.

One of the best things we can do going into the New Year is to take stock of our lives and reflect on where we have been and where we need to go. With God, no matter what, we can always begin again any day of the year!

January 12, 2012

What God Wants From Us

When I found your words, I devoured them; they became my joy and the happiness of my heart. – JEREMIAH 15:16

I know it is more complicated than this, but it seems that church people fall into three basic categories: dabblers in religion, religious fanatics and serious disciples.

Dabblers in religion are those who are afraid to really commit and afraid not to, both at the same time. They go "through the motions" of religious observance, but they never "put away the old self and put on the new self" that St. Paul talks about in his letter to the Ephesians.

Religion is just one more good thing they "should get involved in, but don't." They may send their kids to a Catholic school, help out at the church picnic and sign up for the parish softball league, but they seldom attend Mass or let their religious beliefs influence the way they choose to live.

Religious fanatics are people who are motivated by an extreme unreasoning enthusiasm. They try to demonstrate their conviction by ramming that conviction down the throats of others. "Holier than thou," their motto is, "Thank God I am not like the rest of humanity." Their favorite bumper sticker is the one that reads, "I'm saved, sorry about you."

In their smug certitude, they specialize in judging others and speaking for God. These people probably drive more people away from religion than any atheist. Unable to inspire, they sometimes turn to political maneuvers to enforce conformity.

Serious disciples are people who are committed to growing into the likeness of the risen Christ. They let their actions, rather than their words, speak for them, making them attractive to believers and non-believers alike.

Having found the "buried treasure" and the "pearl of great price," they are driven to enter the kingdom of God, not only when they are dead, but now, while they are here. Their lives are marked by fidelity, compassion, patience, kindness and simple goodness. Having found God's words, they devour them, becoming their joy and the happiness of their hearts.

We grow to resemble the God we believe in. If we believe that God is judgmental and vindictive, that's the God we teach and preach and that's what we will become: judgmental and vindictive. If we believe in a merciful, compassionate God who loves us without condition, that's the God we teach and preach, and that's what we become: merciful, compassionate and loving toward all people. We grow to resemble the God we believe in.

What God wants from us is our hearts. In the words of St. Paul, he wants us to "devour his words and have them become our joy and the happiness of our hearts." He wants us to hunger and thirst for holiness. He wants to be taken seriously. He wants a relationship. He wants to be part of our decision making.

September 18, 2003

Unhealthy Dependency

There are many parts, but one body.
1 CORINTHIANS 12:20

A friend of mine lost her husband recently. A few days after the funeral, I called to ask how she was doing. I am still carrying her extremely insightful answer around in my head: "I knew who I was when he was here. Now I don't."

I have been trying to understand why those words resonated so deeply with me. I think I know. Retirement is exactly two years away this month. It occurred to me that I could be saying the same words to myself in a little different way when that day rolls around. I know who I am as a very active priest, but will I know who I am when the pace dramatically slows down?

I am beginning to realize that I am so enmeshed in priesthood that there is practically no difference between "Father Knott" and "Ron Knott." I realize that I will be a "priest forever" theologically, but in reality my identity will change significantly upon entering retirement. Some priests, like widows and widowers, are so unprepared for that transition that they are left feeling totally lost, while others thrive in their new identity.

Most of us find our identity in our relationships, and when those familiar relationships change or end, we feel lost and do not know who we are. Some seem to manage those changes and losses better than others.

Many people find it hard to successfully moderate the forces of individuality and togetherness that mark their relationships.

Too much aloneness can lead a person to disconnect from those around him, while too much togetherness can lead a person to helpless dependency. Too much dependency on other people is called "enmeshment." Merging totally into one's vocation could also be a form of "enmeshment."

"Enmeshment" means being entangled with another person or one's vocation to the point of becoming dependent upon them for the totality of one's emotional needs. It is when you are so close or so involved that you don't know where you end and they begin.

A businessman who cannot take time away from his work to be with his family could be called "enmeshed." A priest who cannot relate to people in any other way than a priest to parishioner could be called "enmeshed." A parent who is overly-involved in the life of their adult child could be called "enmeshed." A marriage partner who is unable to engage in independent thought could be called "enmeshed."

People without a core sense of self cannot usually maintain healthy relationship either, for that matter. They become so clingy and suffocating that they make the object of their desire feel so oppressed that they have a need to run away. As I like to tell couples who come to me for marriage, "Two half-people have never made a happy couple, any more than a half-person an effective priest."

October 18, 2012

The Good Left Undone

Teacher, all of these I have observed from my youth.
MARK 10:17-27

Before Catholics stopped going to weekly confession in great numbers, we used to hear confessions for at least an hour every day in one parish where I served. It was the place where people came to be deliberately anonymous.

Most of those confessions would put you to sleep; some would move you to tears and a few would spontaneously curl the hair on your head. The penitents who would irritate were not those who returned week after week having done the same old thing over and over, but the ones who confessed this way: "Bless me, Father, I don't know what to tell you. I didn't take the name of the Lord in vain. I didn't gossip. I didn't miss Sunday Mass. I didn't commit adultery. I didn't steal anything. My parents are dead, so I didn't disobey or disrespect them."

What was irritating was their belief that sin is only about doing bad things, and so their discipleship was reduced to simply avoiding bad things. They were like the rich young man who was able to say to Jesus, "I have observed all these commandments since my youth. I never did this! I never did that! I never did such and such!"

Unlike sinful me, Jesus did not get irritated by this young man's confidence in his ability not to break the commandments. It says that Jesus "looked at him with love." But after the kind smile, Jesus hit him between the eyes with a challenge: "Yes, you have avoided evil and that is good, but now do something great, do something positive, do something heroic. Let go of the thing you trust the most – your financial security – and trust me instead."

It says that "his face fell," and he "went away sad" because he couldn't "let go" of his "many possessions." He could avoid the bad thing, but he couldn't do the great thing.

The "Confiteor" is part of an ancient penitential rite in the Mass. It is an option that is regaining popularity, especially among young seminarians. It is still used in many places on a regular basis. In the Confiteor, we confess the bad we have done as well as the good that we have left undone. Very often we do not perpetuate horrible evils on each other nearly as much as we fail to do great things.

Maybe Edmund Burke summarized our sin best when he said, "All that is necessary for the triumph of evil is for enough good people to do nothing." Maybe the real problem of our church and world is not the handful of infamous evil people doing dreadfully bad things, nearly as much as the hordes of ordinary good people doing nothing great.

There is a lot more to Christianity than keeping our own noses clean. We probably sin more in the area of "what we have failed to do" than "what we have done."

March 30, 2006

To Curse or To Bless

All bitterness, fury, shouting and reviling must be removed from you, along with malice. Be kind to one another, compassionate, forgiving one another. – EPHESIANS 4

In the Book of Deuteronomy, God invites us to choose between a blessing or a curse, between doing good or doing evil, between blessing others or cursing them, between wishing them well or wishing them harm.

In many ways, we have become a nation of cursers instead of blessers. Television, music, movies and magazines are crammed with four letter words. Drive down any highway and you will see people cursing each other with flying fingers and flailing fists. Visit almost any school and you will see kids cruelly taunting, teasing and cursing each other, even little kids. The act of cursing has become so prevalent in our society that we seem to be surprised when people bless each other.

To bless means to wish total and unconditional good for others. It means to hold others in reverence, to invoke divine care upon them, to acknowledge and affirm their basic goodness, to think or speak positively about them, to wish them happiness.

Cursing is the opposite of blessing. To curse is to call evil or injury down on someone. It is to invoke evil or pray for bad to happen.

We have a choice between blessing and cursing, between calling down goodness and calling down evil. As Christians,

Paul tells us that if we are to live a life worthy of our calling, we must learn the spiritual practice of blessing people.

Beauty is truly in the eye of the beholder. What you see is what you experience. As you look at the world, you can look at people and see problems and failures, or you can look at people and see buried treasure and hidden beauty. As you look at people you can choose either to bless them or to curse them.

We are invited to adopt the spiritual practice of blessing people. When I look for material for this column, I like to take a position where I can really observe people. I try to "feel with them." I try to imagine the burdens they are carrying and the problems they are facing and then call down God's blessings on them. I believe that when I do this, goodness is called down on them. It is best when they don't know I am doing it.

We are invited to adopt the spiritual practice of blessing people. When you pass people on the street, in their places of work or play, in school or at home, bless them. Call down God's goodness on them. When you meet or talk to people, in the stillness of your heart, bless them in their health, their work and their relationships.

Finally, when you look in the mirror every morning, bless that person staring back at you. Don't beat him/her up and then send him or her off to work. Instead, say: "God bless you, today."

November 9, 2006

A Poverty That's Within Us

The works of the flesh are rivalry, jealousy, selfishness and factions. The fruits of the Spirit are joy, kindness, generosity and fidelity. – GALATIANS 5:19-23

In a culture where obesity is a major health concern, it is not surprising that one of our most popular TV shows is "The Biggest Loser."

Teams of overweight people commit themselves to a modern version of a "fat farm" to compete with each other in losing weight.

People who are not serious or successful get voted off the show each week until all but the winners have been eliminated. Many people experience a life-saving change – so there are several positive things one could say about this hit program.

Closely related, but maybe not as healthy, is our culture's obsession with things such as liposuction, Botox injections, implants and cosmetic surgery. Though these are often risky and mainly for aesthetical purposes, I suppose there are some situations where even these drastic measures can be beneficial to some people.

Similar to all this is tattooing and body piercing, whereby one can personalize one's exterior according to one's taste. This option ranges from the tasteful to the grotesque. Like all trends that come and go, this one will surely run its course in due time.

If I were wanting to invest in a something with a future, I would surely invest in a tattoo removal and reconstructive surgery clinic to remove neck and face tattoos and to sew up over-stretched ear lobes.

What looks "hot" in one's twenties looks like "a cry for help" in one's sixties. As an email I received recently put it, the following things just don't "work" together: nose rings and bifocals, pierced tongues and dentures, ankle bracelets and corn pads, a belly button ring and a gall bladder surgery scar, Speedos and cellulite.

It is obvious to me that we are obsessed in our culture with making external changes as a path to happiness, when the real path to happiness is through making internal changes. Instead of ranting and raving against our culture's obsession with material things, maybe we need to make a better case for looking inside, rather than outside. Exploring this inner path to happiness is called "spirituality," the constant breaking through of our awareness to the connection we have with ourselves, with one another and with God.

Before launching his public ministry, Jesus struggled with which direction to take – outer world or inner world. He rejected all the "outer world" options presented to him by the devil and chose, rather, to explore the "inner world," summarized by the first word out of his mouth – *metanoiete*. Instead of telling us to "change things," he told us to "change the way we see things," to "change our whole value system."

Mother Teresa nailed it when she said that poverty in America is worse than the poverty of India because it is internal. She tried to warn us that many materialistic cultures before us have died from the vacuum within.

July 16, 2009

Principles for Examining Your Life

A voice shall sound in your ears; "This is the way; walk in it, when you would turn to the right or the left." – ISAIAH 30:24

Have you ever taken the time to sit down and assess some of the principles you live by? Socrates said that "the unexamined life is not worth living."

I don't know if that is true in the absolute sense, but I do believe that people who do examine their lives, who think about where they have been, where they want to go and the paths they need to follow to take control of how they want to live their lives, are much happier people. Instead of living on "automatic pilot," following a "whatever happens, happens" pattern, there is a better way.

When you set aside time to examine your life, you have a much better probability of getting to choose your destination, to determine your path and to take control of what you want to be instead of being a victim — a victim of circumstances and a victim of other people's choices for you.

These are a few of the life principles that I have adopted and try hard to practice:

1. *God loves you, without condition, regardless of what you have done or failed to do.* Some grow up believing that God loved them when they were good, quit loving them when they were bad and started loving them again when they shaped up.

This last belief inevitably keeps God at a distance, but God becomes a trusted daily companion with the other belief.

2. *People may treat you badly, call you names, abuse you or try to block your growth*. Those things may hurt, but they only become problems if you start believing that you deserve to be treated that way. Treat yourself with the greatest respect, regardless of how you are treated.

3. *Do not let your fears rule your life*. The only way to overcome fear is to stand up to your own cowardice and face it down. Do hard things for your own good. You are more able than you think you are, and with God's grace, you are capable of things you have hardly imagined.

4. *Everybody craves love, driving them sometimes to look for it in all the wrong places*. Decide to be a love-giver no matter how needy you feel, and you will be showered eventually with all the love you need. Be proactive with your generosity, without any concern for thanks or appreciation, and your generosity will eventually come back to you a hundred-fold. Practice random and anonymous acts of kindness. You reap what you sow, be it good or evil.

5. *Keep no enemies and hold no grudges*. Make peace if you can, and if you can't, let it go before it eats a hole in your soul. "Holding onto anger is like grabbing a hot coal with the intent of throwing it at someone else; you are the one who gets burned."

November 11, 2010

Finding Holiness in Your Marriage

Love does not seek its own interests.
1 CORINTHIANS 13:5

During my 37 years of being a priest, I have met many good married people who truly "hunger and thirst for holiness." In more cases than not, they look to become holy by mimicking the spirituality of religious communities, even to the point of becoming associate members.

There is certainly nothing wrong with that, and there is certainly much to be learned from religious communities. But marriage itself is meant to help marriage partners attain holiness in their married life and in welcoming and educating their children.

Obviously, the church needs to do a better job of encouraging marriage partners to look within their own marriages to find their holiness.

In a fascinating passage in the *Catechism of the Catholic Church*, we are told: "There are two sacraments that are directed toward the salvation of others — Matrimony and Holy Orders. If they contribute as well to personal salvation, it is through service to others that they do so."

Just as priests are made holy through serving others as teachers of the Word, ministers of the sacraments and leaders of the community, married people are made holy by becoming good spouses and good parents. Both married couples and priests become holy through their service to others, not by mimicking the spiritualities of others.

The sacrament of marriage gives spouses the grace to mediate the love of Christ to each other, strengthens their indissoluble unity and gives them strength in welcoming and educating children, making them holy in the process.

With Christ dwelling in them, the sacrament of marriage gives married couples the strength they need to endure suffering, to recover after they have fallen, to forgive one another and to bear one another's burdens.

Our culture is forever teaching people that they marry for what it can do for them. As the old Toyota commercial put it, "I love what you do for me." In an old newspaper clipping I have in my "marriage homily file," the woman who held the record on the number of times she had been married put it this way: "All I ever wanted was someone to love me."

The church teaches something quite different. The church teaches us that marriage, one of the sacraments of service, is entered into for the good of others. They marry not so much to be loved as to mediate love to each other, to their children and to the community at large. Maybe the poor woman cited above would have had better luck if she had married to be a benefit to her partner?

With all this said, maybe the best way for marriage partners to become holy is not to "act religious" or "wear their piety on their sleeves," but to devote themselves to being the best spouses and parents they can be, by focusing on being the best people they can be and on what they have to offer their partners and children.

October 25, 2007

Two Becoming One

Be united in the same mind and the same purpose.
1 CORINTHIANS 1:10

Catholics tend to think that marriage and priesthood are polar opposites, when in reality they have much in common. Both marriage and priesthood have a radical communitarian dimension. Just as "being married and acting single" is a distortion of marriage, a priest in "private practice" is a distortion of priesthood.

Marriage has a radical communitarian dimension. Two individuals become a community of persons through a promise of total and mutual self-giving for each other's good and for the good of the children who come from their union. In the process of "two becoming one," marriage partners do not give up their own preferences and points of view, but they do give up an over-attachment to them. For the sake of their marriage unity, they pledge to think "we," not just "me."

Ordained ministry has a radical communitarian dimension. For that to be possible, each and every priest makes a promise of obedience, a covenant of sorts, with the bishop and every other priest in the presbyterate not to be overly attached to his own preferences and points of view for the sake of a coherent and unified ministry to the people of God. Like marriage partners, priests do not give up their individual preferences and points of view, but they do pledge to give up an over-attachment to them. They pledge to think "we," not just "me," for the sake of their shared ministry.

Since both marriage and ordained ministry hold individuality and communality in a delicate balance, it might be good to suggest a simple template on how that might be done —how two or more might be one. I borrowed this template from Pope Paul VI's document on ecumenism, *Ecclesiam Suam.*

Agreement on the essentials: In marriage, as well as priesthood, there are a few things that are non-negotiable, but what those issues are needs to be spelled out clearly rather than assumed. Problems occur when essentials are treated as non-essential and non-essentials are treated as essential. Clarity of facts is vital.

Meekness and respect in dialogue: If "a communitarian dimension" and "a unity of purpose" are to be maintained in marriage and priesthood, one has to monitor one's speech. This means the avoidance of arrogance, barbed words and bitterness, an individual patience with contradictions, an inclination toward generosity and magnanimity and acceptance of the fact that divergent views often serve to complete each other.

Consensus on non-essentials: Unity is impossible without a "give-and-take" on things that are not essential. Having an opinion, a preference and a point of view is not the problem, but once cooperative discernment has taken place, one has to resist an over-attachment to one's opinions, preferences and points of view and accept co-responsibility for directions to be taken and choices made. Such a healthy "give-and-take" can lead to a universal acceptance of a workable and reasonable, even if not perfect, plan for going forward.

July 26, 2012

Cultivating Virtue - Prudence

The prudent man looks where he is going.
PROVERBS 14:15

In this year's Lenten series, I have pledged an internal rather than an external focus. I have promised to focus on doing something positive, rather than [the practice of] "giving up" things — on "cultivating virtues," to be precise.

"Virtue" comes from the Latin word "virtus," meaning "strength" or "power." Virtues are qualities of the mind, the will and the heart that instill strength of character and stability of personality. A virtue is acquired by repetition and practice. A virtuous person, then, is a creature of habit, a person who not only knows and values what is good, but also one who has the ability to choose that good in consistent, concrete actions.

One of the habits of a virtuous person is prudence. Prudence helps us make good decisions. Prudence is the ability to perceive reality as it really is and then to make good decisions in accordance with that perception. Prudence allows us to choose what is truly good and reject what is truly bad. The consistent habits required to develop the virtue of prudence are deliberation, judgment and decision.

Before a person can be said to possess prudence, he must be able to gather information and analyze it critically. Confusing fact and fiction has become commonplace in our culture. A prudent person is a dealer in truth. This means assessing the reliability of sources and distinguishing between facts and opinions, truth and half-truths.

A prudent person not only loves the truth, he also refrains from his own rationalization — attempts to make true what he loves, twisting reality to fit his own preconceived notions. A prudent person knows that "the truth will set you free," no matter how painful it is to face. A prudent person is also able to see through his own prejudices. Rationalization has its roots in cowardice. Prejudice stems from ignorance. Both keep us from dealing in truth.

Prudence, then, involves both the ability to see reality as it is before we act as well as reality as it will be after we have acted. Maybe this aspect of prudence is the most in need of revival in our culture.

We live in a culture where decisions are often made quickly, without solid information and without serious reflection on their consequences. Impulse buying that leads to financial ruin, casual sex that leads to unwanted pregnancies and venereal disease, impetuous decisions to marry that lead to divorce, and a general rush to judgment that leads to a host of unwanted consequences are only a few of the consequences that we have to live with when we lack prudence.

Having good intentions and meaning well, as popular as they are, are not good enough for a serious disciple. Prudence is the ability to discern what is truly good and to choose that good in consistent, concrete actions.

Lent is a time to slow down, to stop, to look and to listen. It is a time to learn prudence.

February 25, 2010

The Virtue of Justice

Give to Caesar what is Caesar's and to God what is God's.
MATTHEW 22:21

Last week, I focused on prudence, the virtue that helps us make good decisions in whatever situation we find ourselves. This week, I want to focus on the second cardinal virtue — justice. Justice is the consistent habit of rendering to each one his due.

The first duty of justice is giving God his due — having no other gods before him. The consistent habits the virtue of justice requires are regular habits of prayer, worship, obedience and upholding any vows we have made. With only 23% of American Catholics attending Mass weekly and many abandoning their vows, it seems that the virtue of justice could use quite a bit of Lenten focus.

The second duty of justice is toward those around us. Here we must not only be willing to refrain from doing them evil, we must actually develop the habit of doing good toward those around us, even to our enemies. We must respect the rights of every person and be willing to promote the equality of all people and to dedicate ourselves to the building up of the common good. The virtue of justice helps us be able to live in community. In a culture that is becoming more individualistic, one that cares less and less about the rights of others, this aspect of the virtue of justice could use some Lenten attention for sure.

Other virtues that derive from the cardinal virtue of justice are piety, obedience, gratitude, veracity, affability and equity.

Piety is about practicing habits of reverence and service to our parents, to our country and to others in legitimate authority. Disrespect for, and neglect of, parents could certainly use some attention during Lent, as well as our obligation to being law-abiding citizens. Cheating — whether it is running red lights, speeding, shoplifting or tax evasion — weakens us as a community and as a country and could use some reflection this Lent as well. In a culture of character assassination, selfish disregard for norms of law and disrespect for legitimate authority, the virtue of piety could certainly use some attention.

Obedience, in the sense of not being overly attached to one's own preferences and points of view, is what holds communities, families, marriages and parishes together. Gratitude, which springs from the certain knowledge that everything is a gift, cannot survive in a culture of entitlement. Telling the truth, whether convenient or inconvenient, is something that can no longer be taken for granted. Affability, being easy to be around, could certainly use some attention when cynicism and nasty behavior are usually expected. Balance, rather than excess, in eating, entertainment and work could certainly use some Lenten attention as well.

March 4, 2010

Fortitude

Nothing in life is more useful than moderation and prudence, justice and fortitude. – WISDOM 8:7

This week, we continue our Lenten focus on cultivating virtues rather than on simply "giving up things" by considering the third cardinal virtue — fortitude.

The virtue of fortitude enables a person to endure the hardships of life and to remain steadfast in the pursuit of what is good. Fortitude strengthens our resolve to resist temptations and to overcome obstacles in living a moral life.

Fortitude is not the same as foolhardiness, which is so popular in today's culture, in which people foolishly risk their lives or take arbitrary chances that have no useful purpose except to draw wanted attention to themselves. Going over Niagara Falls in a barrel is nothing compared to the fortitude it takes to live with cancer, or any other chronic disease, without losing heart.

Fortitude does not make a person immune from fear. Instead, a person with fortitude recognizes fear, but does not allow fear to prevent him from doing what is good. Sometimes that fear will make a person do what is evil out of peer pressure. Fortitude enables one to conquer fear, even fear of death, and to face trials and persecution. Fortitude even helps one sacrifice his life in defense of a just cause.

In its simplest form, fortitude strengthens one's ability to endure over the long haul, to deal with setbacks and to finish a job. Fortitude is marked by patience, which inclines a person to endure present hardships, and perseverance, which inclines a person to continue steadfastly in the pursuit of virtue. The opposites of fortitude are cowardice, recklessness, timidity, fickleness and boastfulness.

Fortitude, then, is the strength of mind that enables a person to encounter danger or to bear pain or adversity with courage. Fortitude, being a cardinal virtue, is one of the most essential virtues for living the Christian life today, whether you are married, whether you are a priest or whether you are single. Being a Catholic Christian today is more about "swimming against the stream" than "going with the flow." As such, it takes great fortitude to resist the temptation to give up and to overcome obstacles in living a moral life.

I instinctively knew, when I was ordained back in 1970, that one of the virtues I would most need to remain steadfast in my vocation would be fortitude. I chose an old Quaker song to remind me of my need of the fortitude I would need to endure over the long haul. It is called "How Can I Keep From Singing." I will sing it again for my fortieth anniversary this coming May 16th. Part of it goes like this:

> Through all the tumult and the strife, I hear the music ringing. It sounds and echoes in my soul; how can I keep from singing?

> What though the tempest 'round me roar, I hear the truth it liveth. What though the darkness round me close, songs in the night it giveth.

March 11, 2010

Temperance

Do not follow your base desires, but maintain your appetites. – SIRACH 18:30

Today, I would like to say a few things about the fourth of the four cardinal or "hinge" virtues — temperance. In previous weeks, I have focused on prudence, justice and fortitude.

The virtue of temperance enables a person to keep his passions in check, moderate his attraction to pleasure and provide balance in the use of the world's goods.

In the end, temperance is about self-preservation. The ability to eat and drink in moderation leads to health. The ability to say "no" to opportunities to commit adultery and fornication leads to the preservation of marriage and family life.

The ability to control one's temper leads to peace in one's heart, in one's family and in one's community. The ability to neither inflate nor devalue one's worth leads to respect for oneself and others. The ability to live with "enough" leads to feelings of satisfaction. The ability to control oneself in the face of excess leads to a sense of personal power.

Intemperance, on the other hand, is about self-degradation and self-destruction. Our society, which honors the virtue of temperance less and less, actually promotes gluttony, drunkenness, impurity, pride, wrath and greed, and it even promotes them as signs of "success." Moderation and self-control are often ridiculed. "Let it out," "go for it" and "you only live once" are regular chants coming from many directions.

Television offers a host of contests, under the heading of "entertainment," that promote gluttonous eating and drinking, sexual promiscuity, "bullying," waste, "getting even" and "winner-take-all" greed. When vice is promoted as virtue and virtue is ridiculed as vice, we are indeed headed for hurt!

The practice and development of the four cardinal virtues are essential to anyone's spiritual life. Saint Augustine spoke about the value of practicing these virtues this way: "To live well is nothing other than to love God with all one's heart, with all one's soul and with all one's efforts; from this it comes about that love is kept whole and uncorrupted (through temperance). No misfortune can disturb it (and this is fortitude). It obeys only (God) (and this is justice) and is careful in discerning things, so as not to be surprised by deceit or trickery (and this is prudence)."

It is not easy for us to maintain moral balance in today's world, but it is still possible even today. Christ offers us the grace necessary to persevere in the pursuit of the virtues — through prayer, through the frequent reception of the sacraments and through the example and intercession of the saints. In the end, we need to be "intentional" about living the moral life. "Intentional" means to "reach for," "to stretch toward."

"Blessed are those who hunger and thirst for righteousness, for they will be satisfied."

March 18, 2010

Some Thoughts About Growing Old

My son, take care of your father when he is old; grieve him not as long as he lives. Even if his mind fails, be considerate with him; revile him not in the fullness of your strength. – SIRACH 3:12-13

I like old people. I especially like feisty old people, the ones who may be old in body but young at heart. Even as a young priest, I was always more comfortable with the parish senior citizen group than I was with the parish youth group.

Not only am I attracted to the energy of old people, but they also are attracted to my energy. In fact, I have been called an "old lady magnet" more than once to my face. Even Archbishop Kelly pointed out to me that I seem to always have a need for "a mother or two" all the time.

The facts make me have to admit that he is right. I have often found myself knee-deep in "mothers," especially when I was a pastor. Even today one of the highlights of my week is Friday morning, my day off, when I go visit my almost 96-year-old friend.

I am not an expert in "senior citizenry," but I have found out a few things about these "golden years" people. The main thing I have discovered is that many people think all they need is a warm bed, a hot meal, a good bath, a few pills and a hasty visit every few months, when in fact they need what all of us need.

What they really need is to be touched, kissed, hugged, held, appreciated, remembered, recognized, consulted, included, respected and trusted.

I turned 60 this year, so I guess about 10 to 15 years from now I ought to start thinking about getting old myself. I already know what kind of old person I want to be when I get there. I want to be one of those feisty old people myself. I want to be one of those old people I enjoy so much — the kind who choose life, the kind who try new things, the kind who push themselves to be engaged, the kind who are focused on others, the kind who milk life for all it's worth.

I sort of look forward to the day when I no longer feel the need to fix everything, but can simply enjoy everything — the day when I can stir up stuff and get away with it; the day when people will think I am cute for doing it.

I agree with Norman Cousins, who said, "Death is not the greatest loss in life. The greatest loss is what dies within us while we live." While I am I admiring those senior citizens who choose to live no matter how old they get, I am learning from them. They are teaching me not to be one of those about whom Nicholas Murray Butler spoke when he said, "Many people's tombstones should read, 'Died at 30. Buried at 60.'"

August 5, 2004

Preparing for the "Golden Years"

How will you acquire in old age what you have not saved in youth? – SIRACH 25:2

I'm not getting any younger, no matter how much I try not to think about it. Next week, I will celebrate my 66th birthday. Is it time to wake up and smell the coffee? It always is.

Actually, I am not so much "in denial" as I am so busy doing what I love that I don't have much time to think about it. The fact that I have at least one sibling older than I am brings a sliver of comfort.

Even more comforting is the fact that I am lucky enough to work around young people all week, which also helps me forget just how old I am. The exception is when they say something like this when I am talking to them about something that seems to me to have happened only a few years back: "Father, I wasn't born till 1983."

For God's sake, that's the year I went to the Cathedral as pastor. That seems to me like yesterday. It doesn't help, either, to get multiple mailings in one day, as I did recently, from the Scooter Store, Medicare, AARP and a couple of burial insurance companies. They certainly know my age and are already salivating for their cut of my retirement funds.

I like to take the occasion of my birthday every year to laugh in the face of age and offer "an encouraging word" to people like myself.

My policy is quite simple — prepare and forget. I even teach young priests-to-be how to set up personal retirement plans early so that they, too, can forget about them until they need them.

Recently, I have been reviewing, organizing and refining my own plan so that I can head into the home stretch without being a burden to the diocese or my family. I even have a nursing care policy in place. When all that has been tweaked, I hope to go on as if I am going to live forever. Barring any major health crises, I want to proceed as if the best is yet to come.

The prayer that best fits me on my 66th birthday is the prayer of Saint Francis de Sales. If you like it, cut it out, keep it and pray it. It's entitled, "Be at Peace."

"Do not look forward in fear to the changes of life; rather look to them with full hope as they arise. God, whose very own you are, will lead you safely through all things; and when you cannot stand it, God will carry you in his arms. Do not fear what may happen tomorrow; the same everlasting Father who cares for you today will take care of you then and every day. He will either shield you from suffering or will give you unfailing strength to bear it. Be at peace and put aside all anxious thoughts and imaginations."

April 22, 2010

An Unconditional Love

Love one another as I have loved you.
JOHN 15:12

Because I grew up with strong feelings of rejection, I have ended up being a "specialist," if you will, in reaching out to alienated and disaffected Catholics. Even if I live to be a hundred, it looks like I will never run out of a job in this arena.

I have heard hundreds of stories of Catholics who simply left the church altogether in anger. I have heard even more stories of Catholics who have chosen to move to another parish because of this or that priest, sister or lay leader. Now I am hearing stories of people who are withholding their contributions to the church because of their anger over our ongoing scandal.

Psychologists tell us that withholding affection is a technique we learn as children to express our anger without having to deal with it directly. Married couples, unable to express anger at each other or their children in an open and constructive way, often use this technique on each other and on their kids. Children, raised with this technique, use it when they grow up. It is a form of emotional abuse. It can be as passive as simply ignoring others or as aggressive as the use of belittling language or the restriction of basic emotional needs.

Recently, I received a letter from an angry family who abandoned their parish because of the remarks of their new pastor. Instead of confronting the priest directly and working through it, they chose "withholding affection." I have a hunch they learned this response to anger and powerlessness when they were children.

Many of us grew up in homes that gave us the message that we were loved conditionally. We learned early that if we did what we were told, we would be accepted. If we failed to do what we were told, we would be shunned, emotionally or physically, until we did.

Unable to talk about anger and disappointment in an open and honest way, we learned to punish each other by "withholding affection." Hundreds of talk show guests tell us that they have not spoken to their parents, siblings or former spouses for years. Anyone who has fallen into that trap knows that it ends up hurting the one who withholds more than it does the one from whom it was withheld.

Some people even believe that God treats us that way. They believe that God loves us when we are good, quits loving us when we are bad and starts loving us again when we shape up. Wrong! God loves us without condition, no matter what we do or fail to do. Yes, we can reject God's love, but God never quits loving us. God never withholds his love for us no matter what we do. We are called to love one another as Jesus loved us: without condition!

December 12, 2002

Sit on God's Front Porch

> While he was still a long way off, his father caught sight of
> him, and was filled with compassion. He ran to his son,
> embraced him and kissed him. – LUKE 15:20

One of the questions priests get regularly is, "Father, what should I do about my adult children?"

Usually the question involves situations about them living together with a partner outside marriage, not going to church, involvement with drugs or alcohol, not having their babies baptized and the like.

Over the years, I have come up with my only bit of advice to parents. It does not always work, nor can it always be applied to small children who need discipline, but I have been surprised at how often it has worked with adult children over whom they have little power anyway.

I tell them to "sit on God's front porch for a while." This idea comes from the parable I quoted above. We often call it the "Parable of the Prodigal Son," but it is better called the "Parable of the Loving Father."

What was the response of the father in this parable to the unwanted, destructive behavior and abrupt departure of his beloved younger son? He sits on his front porch and prays and keeps his eye on the driveway for any sign of him coming to his senses. It doesn't say how long he waits, but we might recall that St. Monica did this for many years over her wayward son, St. Augustine.

When the son hits bottom, comes to his senses and realizes he has no place to go except back home, he is not met with "I told you so. I hope you learned your lesson. I knew you would come crawling back. You have no idea how much you have disappointed me and your mother."

It says the father — realizing that his son had come to his senses, learned his lesson, will have to live with the consequences of his bad judgment and does not need to have it rubbed in — welcomes him back with open arms!

He does it without folded arms, cold frowns, thumping feet, piercing stares, but with kisses and hugs. His gushing responses contrast with his older sibling's pouting, withholding and punishing self-righteousness.

If you have a child, brother, sister or friend who has "been gone" following a path of self-destruction and you don't know what to do after exhausting all your pleas and offers of help, try "sitting on God's front porch" for a while. Pray, wait, keep your heart open and be ready to open your arms, no matter how wounded they may be.

When it comes to brothers and sisters, nieces and nephews, parishioners and friends, I have always tried to treat them as I would want to be treated — with the love of the father in this parable, with the same love that God extends to me when I make mistakes, choose badly and let myself and others down.

May 23, 2013

An Incredible Message

He gave everybody a full day's pay.
MATTHEW 20

Of all the parables of Jesus, this is one of my very favorites. A parable is a little, made-up story to make a point about God. Jesus came to reveal God, and because his audience was made up of simple people, he made up little, pointed stories as a way to get his message across. It was a way to help them understand something they didn't know by comparing it to something they did know.

The point that Jesus makes about God here is that God is nuts about us. The hero in this little parable is a vineyard owner. Jesus' listeners were familiar with vineyard owners, but the owner in this story seems a little crazy. You know what this owner did? He gave all his workers, even those who came in at quitting time, a full-day's pay no matter how much or how little they worked for him.

There were two different audiences listening to Jesus, and he wanted both to hear him. He spoke to the "religious types," the ones who kept all the rules, and to the "non-religious types" who couldn't, wouldn't or hadn't kept the rules.

This message outraged the "religious types" who thought that God should love them more because of all they had done for God. To them it was bad news. It was unfair. The "non-religious types" were bowled over to hear that God loved them with all his heart, in spite of the fact that they had done so little for God. To them it was good news. It was not about fairness, but generosity.

If Jesus wanted us to know that God loves us no matter how much or little we do for him, that a pretty mind-blowing message. It sounds unbelievable, too good to be true. Because it sounds too good to be true, many cannot accept it. They say he must not have meant what he said. So, let us help it make sense by adding a list of "yes, buts," playing down the radicalness of this mind-blowing good news, saying "Yes, God loves you unconditionally, but, if, when, except."

The reason so many religious types are threatened by this parable is their fear that if people start believing that, they will do anything they please.

They believe that what people really need is the fear of God. Fear is what will keep them in line, these people say. But what really happens is when people finally "get" this incredible message is really the opposite. People want to change their lives. They will "hunger and thirst" for holiness in the broadest sense of the word.

How about you? Do you believe the message of this parable? Do you "get it" – that God already loves you? Once you accept that, once you begin to live out of that knowledge, God will slowly turn your life around. You will begin, maybe for the first time in your life, to love God, your neighbor and yourself with all your heart.

November 10, 2005

The Hound of Heaven

As a young man marries a virgin, your Builder shall marry you; and as a bridegroom rejoices in his bride so shall God rejoice in you. – ISAIAH 62:5

Many people have an image of God like the one in the Book of Daniel – an old man, with a white beard, sitting on a golden throne. As an old man, he simply sits on a throne presiding over creation. That God is "up there" and "out of our way," looking at us from a safe distance. That God is an observing, but rather passive, God, a God who is easy to ignore, at least for now.

There are, however, other images of God that are actually more common, images of a God who wants passionately to be involved in our lives.

Many passages use "bedroom language" to describe this kind of God. These images of God are seldom referred to because they are unsettling to religious types. Take the words *el kana*. *El* means God in Hebrew. *El kana* is usually sometimes translated as "*jealous* God." It is better translated as "God who offers wildly passionate love." *El Kana* is a God dripping with sexual energy stalking his beloved human beings like a high school boy does his sweetheart. This God makes religious types, as well as those who would like to dismiss God altogether, very, very nervous.

The God of the Old Testament is actually more like a lusty teenager than an old man. The God of the Old Testament wants a response from us. When we reject God's advances, the word for our rejection in Hebrew is *sane*, a word that means to "feel a revulsion," as when a wife turns away in disgust from her husband's sexual advances. When we turn away from God, we are called *awon*, "frigid." This is why we never hear too much about these images of God. It is much safer to talk about an old man on a throne. It is much safer to talk about a God who simply views us from afar than a pushy young God who can't keep his hands off us!

The message is simple and bold. God wants to get involved with us and play a serious role in our lives. God wants a relationship. Our God does not demand perfection of us; he does not even demand a smooth relationship; he does not seem to care that we fail sometimes, but he does want a continuous response. The worst response we can give God is not failure, but an *awon* response – a frigid response, a cold shoulder, a turning away in disgust to his loving advances.

The closest thing in modern literature to this image of God is Francis Thompson's wonderful "Hound of Heaven." Instead of a lusty teenager panting for his beloved, Francis Thompson uses the image of a hound dog. This "hunting dog" God wants to smother us with kisses and lick us all over as we try to run away.

August 30, 2007

Finding God in the "Thin Places"

The heavens opened and he saw the Spirit of God descending on him. – MATTHEW 3:16

They say that our polluting ways have caused "holes" in the delicate ozone layer, which keeps us from being fried by the sun's radiation.

In the spiritual world, there are similar "holes" in the dense layer that veil our view of God. Instead of deadly rays from the sun, a little of God himself shines through.

The Irish call them "thin places," places where the separation between heaven and earth, the sacred and the secular, seems especially porous. God leaks through more easily in these places, it is thought. Another way of saying it is that, in such places, people find the presence of God more easily. I, too, have been in such places where God seemed especially present.

Before she died at age 98, I used to fix a Mother's Day brunch every year for an old friend who was not even kin to me. It was always a magic time, a time when I felt that I was actually mediating God's love to someone who needed to feel it in a tangible way. On such occasions, it was obvious from her face that these simple gestures had great significance.

When I was on-call at the neonatal unit of Norton Hospital, I was called in the wee hours of the morning by the parents of a very sick child. When I got there, I found them asleep on the floor, face to face, holding one rosary between them, obviously exhausted from several nights of keeping vigil. They had fallen asleep praying for God's help. I could feel the presence of God hovering over them.

I remember being called to anoint a young man who was dying from the complications of AIDS. It was back when AIDS was new on the scene and people were still reacting irrationally. His family, most of his friends and probably his insurance company had abandoned him, with the exception of one compassionate neighbor. The apartment was almost empty, except for a mattress on the floor.

When I arrived, he was filled with guilt, self-loathing and irritation at the church. He was both repulsed and attracted by the idea of a priest coming to see him. I talked to him about the Jesus I knew, the Jesus who welcomed, touched and ate with the marginalized.

At some point, I put my prayer book down and spoke from the heart. As I tried to comfort him with the "good news" that God loves all of us without condition — no ands, ifs or buts about it — I had a strong sense of Jesus speaking through me at that moment.

There are "thin places" everywhere, places where God seems to leak through more easily. Once we have been under one of these "thin places," we do not need "proof" of the existence of God. We understand on some deep level that God's love is shining on us all the time.

October 11, 2007

Reformation and Transformation

Stop turning my Father's house into a marketplace.
JOHN 2

In a moment of great humility, something rare for our church at that time, the bishops of Vatican II admitted that the church is "semper reformanda" — "always in need of reform." The human side of the church, just as all human organizations, has a tendency to fall into sin and decay and must be called back to fidelity, over and over again, as it moves through history.

In the above reading, which depicts a dramatic and public gesture of outrage, Jesus' anger boils over. It is very important to remember that the anger of Jesus was not directed at people who sinned or failed in all their everyday ways. His anger was directed at those who controlled religion and used it to abuse simple people.

He had pity and compassion on the outcasts, the sick and sinner, but he was outraged at what had happened at the hands of their leaders to the religion he loved. In some of the most blunt words from the mouth of Jesus ever recorded, he called them "snakes, fakes and frauds." He called the places of worship "whitewashed tombs … all clean and pretty on the outside, but filled with stench and rot on the inside."

It is important to note that Jesus was not against organized religion, but what these people had done to organized religion.

As this Gospel story tells us, he did not come to tear down the temple; he simply came to clean house. The temple had become a marketplace, and they were making a profit in every corner of it.

It is sad that many people never see beyond the packaging when it comes to religion. They see only the earthenware jar and never the treasure it holds. The purpose of religion is to serve, not be served. The purpose of organized religion is the transformation of people, not using people to serve organized religion.

It is also sad that many people naively assume that organized religion is evil simply because it has gotten off track here and there in history. Jesus was clear that he did not come to destroy organized religion but to lead it back to its original purpose.

Without organized religion, we would not have the sacred Scriptures, we would be split into millions of personal opinions and small little cults, and we would not have a way to offer support to other believers around the world. Yes, the church may need a good "house cleaning" every now and then, but the organization of the church is always needed.

As Kenneth Woodward has pointed out, for the last 30 or 40 years people have operated out of a romantic notion that all the ills of the church reside with the institution — so that if only we could reform it, we ourselves would be better Christians. The truth quite often is the other way around. The institution will get better when each one of us is reformed and transformed.

October 23, 2003

The Early Church

Their disagreement was so sharp that Paul and Barnabas separated. – ACTS 15:39

The family picture album is a very important part of remembering and sharing family histories: births, baptisms, First Communions, confirmations, birthdays, graduations, anniversaries, Thanksgivings, Christmases, Halloween parties, vacations and proms.

As wonderful as a family picture album is, it never tells the whole story. Unless your family was weird, you never grabbed the camera to get a shot of Mom when she was diagnosed with cancer, a shot of Dad in a drunken rage, uncles and aunts not speaking to each other, old girlfriends who didn't work out, or the looks on your parents' faces when your unmarried sister got pregnant.

The Acts of the Apostles is an album of snapshots of the early church. We read that beautiful passage about everybody meeting for prayer and the breaking of bread, sharing everything in common and attracting members every day. Acts, unlike most family albums, is disarmingly honest.

Not everything was sweetness and light, and if we keep reading, we will see that other side of the very early church.

We have bickering. We read that people sold their possessions and divided them according to each one's need, but we also read that the Greek-speaking widows complained that the Hebrew-speaking widows were getting a disproportionate share of that division.

We have cover-ups. Ananias and Sapphira sold their property and gave it to the church, holding back some of the proceeds, and then lied about it. They both dropped dead.

We have fanaticism. Saul was rounding up Christians and having them jailed for heresy, even holding the coats of those who stoned St. Stephen to death.

We have corruption. Simon, amazed that the Holy Spirit was being conferred by the laying on of hands, saw a gold mine of opportunity. He offered money for that power.

We have confrontation. Paul calls Peter "two-faced" for acting one way around Jewish converts and another around Gentile converts.

These are a few of the not-so-flattering snapshots of the early church that Scripture has the courage to include.

We read about Paul and Barnabas taking young John Mark with them on one of their missionary trips. If you stopped reading at that passage, you would miss the fact that John Mark got cold feet and came home.

On the next trip out, Barnabas wanted to forgive John Mark and try him again. Paul refused. They had a few strong words, and behold, the first team ministry ended in a fight. Unable to resolve their disagreement, Paul and Barnabas split up.

If we imagine the church was perfect in its infancy or during some period in our recent history, we can actually get a distorted picture of the church today. I believe those who criticize the church because it is "not like it used to be" simply do not know how the church "used to be." The fact is the church is "semper reformanda" — "always in need of reform."

May 19, 2005

When Panic Strikes

Peace be with you!
JOHN 20

Last autumn I was sitting on my front porch with a cheap cigar and a yellow pad making some notes for a homily when I noticed a young man crossing the street to check out a yard sale. He was wearing those baggy pants barely covering his rear end with his underwear almost totally exposed. As he ran across the four lanes of traffic of Eastern Parkway, he was tugging with one hand in a half-hearted attempt to keep them up. The next time I looked up he was about to come back across the street with his yard sale bargain, a large portable TV set.

He made it out into the middle of Eastern Parkway with his new TV when, honest to God, his pants fell down around his shoes. Like a deer caught in the headlights, he froze in place as the traffic came toward him from both directions. Not knowing what to do, you could almost see his mind working through his limited options.

Well, he kept his cool, held onto his TV and calmly shuffled to the curb with his pants down around his shoes.

I had to admire his *sophronismos*. *Sophronismos* is one of my very favorite Greek words. It has been translated by some as "knowing what to do in the face of panic."

When I was almost kicked out of the seminary during my second year and my life-long dream of being a priest was headed for the ditch, I needed *sophronismos*, the knowledge of what to do in the face of panic. Somehow God gave it to me.

When I got my first assignment, associate pastor of seven mission churches in Eastern Kentucky, I needed *sophronismos* and God gave it to me.

When I was pastor of the Cathedral of the Assumption and it cracked down two sides during the renovation and almost fell to the ground in a heap of rubble, I needed *sophronismos* and God gave it to me.

Today, the whole church needs *sophronismos*, and maybe you are going through a crisis of your own as well. Maybe you are facing a cancer diagnosis, an unwanted pregnancy, the death of a spouse, the loss of a child, the loss of a job or the end of a relationship. If so, you may need *sophronismos*.

Whatever it is, God offers us even more than *sophronismos*, he offers us peace.

The peace that Jesus offers us when we end up in one of these crises does not always come with the magic fixing of the situation. But it provides us a way to be in that situation. Peace is not the absence of problems, but the certain knowledge that, in the end, things are going to turn out OK. If you have that knowledge, that peace, no storm can knock you off totally off balance.

It is there, in the place of *sophronismos* and peace, that Jesus offers us a place of rest and hope between one panic attack and the next.

July 17, 2003

The Gift of Peace

Have no anxiety at all, but in everything make your requests to God. Then the peace of God will guard your hearts and minds in Christ Jesus! – PHILIPPIANS 4

The dictionary defines anxiety as a "state of intense, often disabling apprehension, uncertainty and fear caused by the anticipation of something threatening." I have made great progress over the years, but I would still describe myself as "anxious." It goes all the way back to childhood, when the "anticipation of something threatening" seeped into my bones.

It is an old wound that has never completely healed. It manifests itself most often when I fall into imagining worst-case scenarios so that I can be prepared to handle them if they do happen. More than 90 percent of my imagined tragedies never happen. I, and a lot of people like me, waste an incredible amount of energy for nothing. Anxiety is a lot like smoking: you know it's bad for you, but it's so hard to stop.

The whole tragedy of anxiety is that it is most often triggered not by what is actually happening, but by what might happen. I might get sick. I might never find a marriage partner. I might not find a job. I might lose my job. I might lose my savings in the stock market. The plane might crash. The boat might sink. The train might wreck. I might get cancer, AIDS or West Nile virus. I might get mugged, raped or robbed. For the anxious person, the possibilities for disaster scenarios are endless.

If Jesus gave us the gift of peace, where is that peace today? If you look around, there are wars, rumors of war, starvation, disease, racism, sexism, ageism, spouse abuse, child abuse, poverty and pollution all around us. The "peace" that Jesus gives us is not the absence of struggle, pain and problems, but an unshakable serenity in spite of, and in the face of, those problems.

How do we have the "peace of Christ" in the midst of fear and worry? We have it by focusing not on what might happen or what is happening, but on what we are sure is going to happen. And what is going to happen? The "good news", the "gospel," promises that when all is said and done, good will triumph over evil. It's not up for grabs. It has already been decided.

The gift of peace is a free gift, a gift only God can give. Because God is in charge and wants us to have a full, peaceful life, we are challenged to acknowledge our anxiety and be prepared to let go of it. St. Paul says it comes to us through prayer. "By prayer and petition, with thanksgiving, make your requests known to God. Then the peace of God will guard your hearts and minds!"

Or as Jesus puts it, "Stop worrying like unbelievers," and "Fear is useless. What is needed is trust."

December 5, 2002

Too Much Baggage

Take nothing for the journey. Stay at whatever house you enter. When people will not receive you, leave that town, shaking its dust from your feet. – LUKE 9

Every year in January, I have the practice of going through my house and getting rid of stuff. Though people have called my house "minimal," I still have too much baggage.

Sometimes my stuff owns me. It has to be cleaned around, boxed, stacked, stored, filed and even insured. I especially hate it when I have to go digging for something at the bottom of all that stuff. I know people who never get rid of anything.

Likewise, we seem to hang onto old memories, hurts, fears, dreads, ideas and regrets even when they drag us down and make us sick. Sometimes these anxieties own us. They are rehearsed, gone over, obsessed about and discussed until they drive us and those around us a little crazy. January is also a good month to clean out our hearts as well as our closets.

Not all of us are first-century missionaries, but the advice Jesus gave his disciples back then can help us 21st-century Christians. Travel light. Be happy with what you have. Let go.

We live in a culture obsessed with material things, with having and owning. Sometimes the having is a prison in itself. The more we have, the more we have to maintain and protect. Fear of losing it all often drains us of time and energy and fills us with anxiety.

"Happy are the poor in spirit." Happy are those who are free from craving, free from the work of keeping, free of the anxiety that comes from the fear of losing what we have and free of the distance that too many things creates between ourselves and others.

Living is one thing, and getting ready to live is another. One of the saddest TV shows I've ever seen was one about the widows of Florida whose husbands worked themselves into an early grave so that they could "really live" some magic day in the future.

Many of us live in a world of never enough: never enough money, never enough friends and never enough time. Unable to appreciate what we have, we put off being happy until some imagined time, person or windfall comes into our lives. *Carpe diem* — seize the day. We have enough to be happy right now, even in the face of problems, if we care to.

So much of our baggage is invisible from the outside. Sometimes the heaviest baggage of all is mental: worry, regret and dread. When we hold onto those things, we fail to seize the day. We live in the past or a day that has not yet arrived.

The source of all that baggage is the inability to let go and trust in God's providence, the inability to do one's best and let go of what did happen or what might happen. That's what Jesus meant by "my peace I leave with you."

January 22, 2004

Choosing the Weak

Woe is me! I am a man of unclean lips. – ISAIAH
I am not fit to be called an apostle. – PAUL
Depart from me for I am a sinful man. – PETER

One of the great disappointments of priesthood has to be that Monday after your ordination and first Mass. As much as you would like to think you are a different person, the truth of the matter is that you wake up feeling just like you did the day before you were ordained. You realize quite quickly that you are basically the same person with the same weaknesses and same sins.

I have never felt "good enough" to be a priest. I often wonder why God picked me. I don't worry too much about God. I know that God has a long-standing practice of choosing the weak and making them strong.

So I don't worry too much about God. But I do worry about what people think, because they expect more out of me than God himself expects of me. Sometimes I think they expect too much. No, God doesn't scare me as much as people's expectations of me.

In the Scriptures we read about a whole bunch of "losers" being picked by God for important work. When Isaiah is called to be a prophet, he tries to beg off by pointing out to God that he is not worthy of such a job because he has a foul mouth and is from a family of foul mouths. God is not fazed by his excuses.

He simply sends and angel to him carrying a hot coal to purify his lips. Does that hurt or what?

When Paul was called, he had actually been killing the followers of Jesus. God knocked him off his high horse, cleaned him up in a bath of grace and said, "You're it!"

When Peter was called, he resisted in shock, asking Jesus to get away from him, calling himself a "sinful man." Jesus simply told him not to be afraid because he had another kind of fishing for him to do.

The Scriptures are full of stories about losers, thieves and idiots being called by God for his work. In every case, God would hear none of their excuses. "It is not you who chose me; it is I who chose you."

Let me end this reflection with one of my favorite quotes from W. H. Murray. "Until one is committed, there is hesitancy, the chance to draw back, always ineffectiveness. The moment one definitely commits oneself, then Providence moves, too. All sorts of things occur to help one that would never otherwise have occurred. A whole stream of events issues from the decision, raising in one's favor all manner of unforeseen incidents and meetings and material assistance, which no man could have dreamed would have come his way."

Forget your unworthiness. Forget your doubt. Forget your inexperience. Forget your fear. When God calls, say, "Here I am. Send me." Your happiness depends on it.

April 5, 2007

Be Open to All Who Enter Your Life

Looking up, Abraham saw three men standing nearby. When he saw them, he ran from the entrance of the tent to greet them. – GENESIS 18

One of the things we should have thought more about before we got into the war in Iraq is the fact that the way people think in the Middle East is not always the way we think in the West. We can't seem to understand that the whole world does not share our values, and when they resist our sharing them, we seem to be shocked.

Our reading today gives us a case in point. If we lived out West in an isolated mountain cabin and we looked up one day to see three men approaching our cabin, we would usher the kids inside and grab our gun. Our first instinct would be to protect ourselves from a threat. If we did not know them, we would no doubt assume, until proven otherwise, that they were up to no good.

If we live in an urban area, we would not think of opening our door to three unknown men who came up on our porch and knocked, especially if we were home alone. We would probably ignore the doorbell, speak to them through a locked screen, make sure we have something handy to protect ourselves or even call the police. If we did not know them, we would no doubt assume, until proven otherwise, that they were up to no good.

In this reading, we see Abraham doing something that we have been warned never to do. In the heat of the day, he is resting in the shade of his tent. When he looks up and sees three men approaching, he runs to meet them, bows down to them, invites them in and treats them like royalty — without even knowing who they are or what they want.

This kind of hospitality is still common among the Middle Eastern nomadic herders of sheep and goats as they try to live much as their ancestors have lived for centuries. Desert nomads, even today, are known for their sumptuous hospitality.

Even in such a situation, biblical hospitality is always a give-and-take proposition. The host knows that strangers always bless them with gifts of their own: news from the outside world, fascinating conversation in a very dull and tedious landscape or maybe a vial of exotic spices from some faraway place. In the case of this reading, Abraham and Sarah hear that they are going to have their first baby even in their advanced age.

I got into writing because of two "angels" appearing unexpectedly in my life: an editor from Crossroads Press and a generous benefactor. Because I was open to their ideas, they keep blessing me.

God undoubtedly has wonderful gifts for you this year. These gifts will very likely be delivered to you by the unlikeliest of people, if you are open to all those who enter your life. This is how God works.

October 18, 2007

Seeing the Poor Among Us

Even dogs used to come and lick his sores.
LUKE 16:21

When I need a walk, I like to head to the White Castle at Eastern Parkway and Preston Street for a cup of coffee. It's always good, I believe, for a priest to get out and walk in his neighborhood to see how "real people" live. Today, I would like to begin a series of columns on what I will call "noticing people."

One recent evening I headed out for my usual walk to the White Castle. After I had my coffee, I started home. All of a sudden, out of the corner of my eye, I recognized a street person, sitting (ironically) on the steps of a bank building.

Like a lot of homeless people, he seemed to be wearing everything he owned in layers. He looked like a huge, swollen bundle of old brown rags with a red face. I believe he is both schizophrenic and an alcoholic. He looked so unhealthy that he appeared almost ready to explode. He was old beyond his years.

I have seen, spoken to and helped this man for years. He was a regular at the Cathedral in the 1980s. When I first met him, I remember him being a very handsome young man. It is sad to see just how far he has fallen into hopelessness.

I usually speak, but this time I intentionally slipped by without notice because I had left home without my billfold. I wanted to buy him a cup of coffee and ask how he was doing, but couldn't without a lot of explanation.

On the way home, my mind went over the questions that so many of us, with any heart at all, ask. "How do I react to such people? What is a good way to help without contributing to their problems or getting hurt?"

The first step to helping these people, I believe, is to notice them. The sin of the rich man in the story about Lazarus is not that he was rich, not that he abused a poor man at his gate, but that he failed to even notice him. You cannot do something about the poor without compassion for the poor, and you cannot have compassion for the poor without noticing them.

Even when you want to help such people, it is not easy. Handing out change on the street corner may alleviate our guilt for a minute, but that can sometimes make problems worse.

Many of these people were dumped on the streets as a result of funding cutbacks in social services. If we really want to help, we need to insist that our country address the causes of homelessness. In the meantime, we can support those who deal with the immediate needs of these people, like funding the work of places such as Sister Kathleen (Sheehan's) St. John Center for the homeless or the Franciscan Shelter House. If we can't do that, we can at least speak to them with respect.

October 5, 2006

Giving Alms

When you give alms, do not blow a trumpet before you to win the praise of others. God who sees in secret will repay you. – MATTHEW 6:2,4

Today I want to write about the third of the traditional spiritual disciplines of Lent: almsgiving. (Last week and the week before, I wrote about prayer and fasting.)

Almsgiving is a religiously motivated giving of money or other resources to benefit those needing them. Often linked to prayer and fasting, it is a prominent feature in several major religions and holds a special place in Jewish and Christian religious practice.

The Hebrew word for alms means both "alms" and "justice," implying that almsgiving restores God's right order, a closing of the gap between the rich and the poor. St. Basil of Caesarea (d. 379) affirmed that the excess wealth of the rich is the property of the poor, and failure to give alms to the poor amounted to theft from them. St. Ambrose of Milan (d. 397) also said that property beyond one's needs belongs by right to those who lack necessities.

Medieval Christians gave their alms to monasteries and cathedral churches because of their ability to organize hospices and food programs for the poor. In the later Middle Ages, the begging orders, such as the Franciscans, were maintained through almsgiving. In contemporary experience, almsgiving has taken the form of personal or organizational support for established charities and an emphasis on addressing the causes of poverty, in addition to alleviating its effects. To give alms is a tangible way to "love God and one's neighbor as oneself." To give alms is to mimic the self-giving of God himself.

Jesus warned us in the Ash Wednesday Gospel that when we give alms, we should try to do it without drawing attention to ourselves or our gifts. He tells us not to be like those who go to the temple and have trumpets blowing and cameras rolling when they make their donations.

In a day where charitable gifts are tax-deductible and rewarded by plaques, trophies, honorary degrees or even having buildings named after the donor, most of us have grown to expect some notoriety to come with our giving. And some are even offended when their gifts are not recognized in such a way. There is nothing wrong with that, but Jesus says that attention from people will be your only reward. If you want God to reward you, keep it between the two of you.

We are called this Lent to "give alms," to be generous with our assets. Anyone who wants to can come up with a million good excuses to avoid giving away a share of his or her blessings. But I am hopeful that many of us will look, rather, for opportunities to give.

The easiest way to give alms is to support those smart organizations who best know how to help the poor. Personal involvement in such organizations is even better. Of course, there is nothing wrong with spontaneous, anonymous and random acts of generosity. This last is one of my personal favorites.

February 24, 2005

Find Your Way to Serve Others

You must wash each other's feet. What I have just done was to give you an example: as I have done, so you must do. – JOHN 13:14-16

When Jesus comes to us in history, he simply restated in a more dramatic way what was true from the very beginning — that we must love God and our neighbors as ourselves. He did not just, of course, talk about it.

He lived it to the very last drop of his blood.

While we were still sinners and undeserving of being loved, he still loved us. He would not let the connection of love between God and us be severed — no matter what we do or do not do.

His life and death, which we celebrate in an intense way during Holy Week, was one great "show and tell" on how much we are loved and cared for. One of his great final "show and tells" is recorded in tonight's gospel. Remember, the whole foot washing thing was a response to an argument among his followers over who was the greatest. After telling them, again and again, that "it cannot be that way with you," Jesus gets down on his hands and feet and does what a slave would do — he washed their feet.

The text is clear. This dramatic gesture is only an "example." Surely, Jesus wants more from us that a yearly ceremonial repetition of this "example." Jesus certainly wants us to translate this "foot washing" into our own language and culture.

When I read this gospel, I do not think of a pope crawling along the floor with a gold pitcher and pressed linen towels, pouring water over the feet of aged cardinals, even though that's beautiful in its own way.

I think of all the readers of this column who carry smelly bedpans in nursing homes. I think of husbands and wives sitting for hours in the waiting rooms of doctors' offices for their partner's chemotherapy treatments.

I think of parents with special needs children who are virtual prisoners of their caretaking regimes. I think of those exhausted men and women who are trying to care for their elderly parents in their home.

The challenge of "foot washing" is to find our own ways to serve each other, wait on each other, notice each other's suffering, put each other's need first and be there for each other — for better or for worse, for richer or poorer, in sickness and in health as our married friends put it. In short, to be like Jesus, we need to get over our need to be loved and learn to give love — to get over our need to be getters and learn to be givers.

Again this year, the message of this gospel story is loud and clear. Our happiness lies in cooperation, not competition. The "sacred cow" of competition will not die easily. We must kill it within ourselves first, or else collectively, it will kill us all in the end.

March 28, 2013

123

Judging Others

The Lord bless you and keep you! The Lord let his face shine upon you, and be gracious to you! The Lord look upon you kindly an give you peace! – NUMBERS 6:24-26

I live on a busy street. You can see the world from my front porch. It walks by, drives by and shuffles by like a marvelous circus parade. It is some of the cheapest entertainment available.

Some passers-by are regulars. Some pass by only once. There is the middle-aged woman with a distended belly who walks like she has had one shock treatment too many. There is the scruffy drunk carrying a beat-up, old guitar who likes to aggravate cars with a few in-your-face chords from an old Elvis tune. There is the screaming married couple, with windows rolled down, who decide to have it out with each other while waiting for the traffic light to change. There is the elderly couple, shuffling hand in hand, savoring every squirrel, baby and flower they pass.

There are the U of L athletes, tanned, lean and rippled with muscle, strutting their stuff, proud as peacocks. There is the African-American nurse's aide from the local hospital with grocery bags in each hand, waiting in the rain for a bus to take her to another day's work at home. Too tired to stand, she sits on a wet set of steps. There is the overweight, well-intentioned, if not short-lived, jogger who huffs and puffs his way to that leaner and trimmer waistline in his mind's eye.

What do you see when you see people like these? Do you judge them or bless them? I am embarrassed to admit that I found myself judging some of these people one day as I sat and watched them go by. I was reminded of a line from the movie "On Golden Pond." Katherine Hepburn says to Jane Fonda when she was terribly frustrated with her aggravating, old father, "If you look closely enough, you will realize that he is doing the best he can." Remembering that line, I decided to bless those who walked by my house and pray for them. Who knows how lonely, scared, abused or stressed they are? "There, but for the grace of God, go I."

Prayer has the power to help those who don't even know you are praying for them. Why break the "bruised reed?" Why quench the "smoldering candle?" Jesus says, "Do not judge and you will not be judged." St. Paul says, "The member who hurts the most needs the most attention."

Judging others, especially those we do not know, is a bad habit that says as much about us as the people we judge. This bad habit can be replaced with the good habit of blessing others. All we have to do is monitor our own thinking, check it and replace it with new thinking. A new world is often only a changed thought away.

October 31, 2002

The Gift of Forgiveness

Wrath and anger are hateful things, yet the sinner hugs them tight. Forgive your neighbor's injustice then when you pray, your own sins will be forgiven. – SIRACH 27:30; 28:2

If you haven't decided on a New Year's resolution, I have a suggestion. For your own good, forgive everybody in your life, no matter what they did or failed to do.

One of the hardest and most liberating things I have ever done was to forgive. For much of my life, I carried a huge sack of resentment from childhood. The older I got, the more resentments I added to my collection until the weight and smell of that huge bag of grudges got so heavy and foul-smelling that it was making me sick. Worn out, I decided one day to find a way to rid myself of it, once and for all. I would have ditched it sooner, but I made the mistake of thinking that I had to have justice, or a least an apology, before I could let it go.

Before I let go of it, I had to want to let go of it. And when I wanted to let go of it, I prayed earnestly for help. I did not pray for my offender to change; I prayed that I would change, that I would change my attitude toward what had happened.

My prayers were answered in stages. The first answer to my prayer was to realize that taking offense was just as bad as giving offense. I had to realize that my response to the one who offended me had been as mean as the original meanness. The second answer to my prayer was something I thought impossible. After acknowledging the hurt, I apologized for my withholding, and sometimes hateful, responses. The third response to my prayer, even after two last-minute, aborted attempts, was that I was given a chance to express my apology and my unconditional forgiveness. I went into the experience in knots. I came out walking on air.

I have told my story many times. The reason I tell it repeatedly is because every time I tell it, someone is inspired to move toward forgiveness. I found out a long time ago that there are many people out there carrying soul-eating resentments. Fixated on their anger, they rehearse their injustices and nurse their wounds, sharing them with anyone willing, or unwilling, to listen. They wait for that apology that doesn't come. They stick to their guns even though those guns keep shooting them in the foot, over and over again. What they don't know is that, with God's help, they can free themselves of all that self-inflicted suffering.

God asks us to forgive 7 times 70 times. It is not about doing God a favor, it's about God wanting to do us a favor. He wants to give us the gift of peace. All we have to do is let go of the need to be right.

January 2, 2003

Peter Forgave Himself

Peter was distressed that Jesus had said to him a third time, "Do you love me?" and said to him, "Lord, you know everything; you know that I love you." – JOHN 21

It is one of life's hardest things to do, forgiving others when they have disappointed and hurt us. But accepting forgiveness from others and forgiving ourselves when we have hurt and disappointed others is quite often even more difficult.

It occurred to me this year, as we read the Easter readings, that Peter and Judas have a lot to teach us in this regard.

Both Judas and Peter denied Jesus. Judas was a traitor, turning Jesus over to those who killed him. Peter failed to stand by Jesus, pretending that he had never even known him. Both later regretted their sins, but with one big difference.

Judas could not forgive himself and committed suicide. I am convinced that Jesus would have forgiven Judas if he had come forward, but Judas never gave Jesus the chance and went down in history as a villain. Peter, on the other hand, stepped forward and accepted Jesus' forgiveness, and thereby came to forgive himself, going down in history as a saint.

My friends, have you ever done some awful, hurtful thing to someone you love? Many people have and are spending their lives in regret, unable to forgive themselves. Maybe they have done it to their parents, their siblings or their children, maybe to a spouse or a close friend, maybe to a coworker or neighbor.

Many have done stupid things to hurt themselves. Maybe they have had an abortion because of irresponsible sex, maybe they have lost their life savings in compulsive gambling, maybe they have destroyed their marriage because of infidelity or ruined their health through addiction or maybe they have killed someone while driving intoxicated or with a gun in a rage or even by accident.

Burdened with their inability to forgive themselves, their lives are often stuck in a cycle of destructive self-hatred. Some kill themselves, little by little, with drugs and alcohol. Sometimes, to relieve the pain of regret, they are driven to take a gun and end their lives or, like Judas, hang themselves in their garage.

Peter reminds us that there is another way: we can forgive ourselves by accepting God's forgiveness. With God's forgiveness, we can go on and make a new start.

My friends, we have all failed as disciples, but the important thing is that we recover like Peter, rather than follow Judas, who could neither forgive himself nor accept God's forgiveness. Even though Peter denied Jesus three times, before witnesses and after pledging never to do such a thing, he meets Jesus on the beach after the Resurrection and affirms three times that he did indeed love Jesus.

After that, Peter the Coward soon became Peter the Brave, Peter the Denier became Peter the Public Witness! Traditionally, in a typical Peter way, we are told that he requested to be crucified upside down.

May 30, 2013

The "Medicine of Mercy"

> While he was at table in his house, many tax collectors and sinners sat with Jesus and his disciples; for there were many who followed him. – MARK 2:15

Judgment and condemnation drive people out of the church. Compassion and forgiveness bring them in. This has been made abundantly clear to me, both from both my reading of the Gospels and from my own personal experience as a pastor.

Some of the most beautiful parables of Jesus were given in response to those who were big on judgment and condemnation. Both Jesus and the Pharisees hated sin, but they disagreed on what to do about it. The Pharisees chose judgment and condemnation. Jesus chose compassion and forgiveness. Sinners fled from the Pharisees and flocked to Jesus.

Through a series of personal conversion experiences, I have come to believe that the "universal and unconditional love of God" is the "good news." I stumbled onto it like a person would stumble on a buried treasure. It was transforming.

I had believed that God's love for us was conditional on our success in keeping the rules. I had mistakenly assumed that God loves us when we are good, quits loving us when we are bad and starts loving us again when we shape up. What I had failed to realize was the fact that God loves us even while we are sinners.

In the parable of the loving father, the father loves the older son who stayed home and kept the rules, but he also loves the son who lived with the pigs.

In the parable of the vineyard workers, the owner of the vineyard gives all his workers a full day's pay, no matter when they started working. In the parable of the lost sheep, the shepherd certainly loves the 99 who do what sheep are supposed to do, but he also loves the sheep who wandered off. In the parable of the wedding feast, the good and bad alike are invited to be part of the wedding party.

When I was the pastor of the Cathedral of the Assumption from 1983 to 1997, I made a conscious decision to preach this "good news." We grew dramatically. I got a lot of credit – too much credit, in fact. What drew them was not the messenger, but the message.

I am troubled by what I see as a mean spirit invading our church, disguised as a crusade for "truth." I agree with their goal, but I reject their methods. They are driving more people out of the church than they will ever bring in. Unable to inspire people to holiness, they are settling for naming sins and condemning sinners. Their harsh condemnation may make them feel righteous, but it doesn't turn many people around.

I like what Pope John XXIII said when he opened Vatican Council II. He said that "nowadays the church prefers to make use of the medicine of mercy rather than severity." The "medicine of mercy" works. "Severity" doesn't.

September 16, 2004

Negative Religion Sells!

I write these few words to encourage you never to let go
of the true grace of God to which I bear witness.

– 1 PETER 5:12

Negativity sells! If you don't believe me, just sit in front of
your television and flip through the channels. Murder, scandal,
rape, destruction, assault, theft, infidelity, deceit and torture are
a few of the subjects that bombard us daily on network and
cable TV. That does not even cover "reality" programs, where
personal humiliation is a common thread.

We can blame "those Hollywood people" all we want, but
the real reason there is so much of it on TV is because it sells,
and it sells because people want it.

Negative religion also sells. In general, I find most religious programming embarrassing. If it's not doom and gloom
and hysterical, it's syrupy, simplistic and corny.

If I wanted to make money preaching on TV, really big
money, I would "go negative," too. I would search the Scriptures
for the most obscure apocalyptic passages — you know, those
scary, impending hellfire and brimstone passages. I would per-
suade my audience that God had personally instructed me as to
their precise meaning.

I would make dire predictions about the future. I would di-
vide people into two groups: sinners and saints. I would sanc-
timoniously put myself and those who agree with me in with
the "saints" and everybody else in with the "sinners."

I would argue the merits of crusades, inquisitions and witch hunts. I would identify a few scapegoat groups to beat up on. I would rant and rave about their sins, especially sins related to sex. The money would roll in. It always does.

But if I really had my own religious TV program, I would not be mean in God's name. I would preach about God's goodness, mercy and unconditional love. I would seek out sinners and talk to them as Jesus talked to them, with respect and kindness. Instead of seeing goodness in some people and evil in others, I would have people recognize that we all need God because there is some evil in the best of people and some goodness in the worst of people.

If I had my own religious program, I would pray that, like Isaiah, I would have "a well-trained tongue so that I might speak a word of encouragement to the weary."

I would pray for healing words, words like those of Julia Cameron: "I wish I could take language and fold it like cool, moist rags. I would lay words on your forehead. I would wrap words on your wrists. 'There, there,' my words would say — or something better. I would murmur, 'Hush' and 'Shh, shh, it's all right.' I would ask them to hold you all night.

"I wish I could take language and daub and soothe and cool where fever blisters and burns, where fever turns yourself against you. I wish I could take language and heal the words that were wounds you have no names for."

January 20, 2005

133

Forgiveness Sets You Free

A wound can be bandaged and an insult forgiven.
SIRACH 27:21

I read that Amazon.com lists 160,510 books on the topic of forgiveness. That's 31,629 more than on sexuality. What does that tell us about the human heart and what it hungers for most?

You haven't experienced freedom unless you have experienced the freedom that comes when you let go of resentments that sear your soul, preoccupy your thoughts and drain your strength. Yet, there are so many people who hug their hurts and nurse their wounds in an all-consuming preoccupation because they cannot "let go."

When they refuse to forgive, they choose to be "right" over being free. Catherine Ponder said it best when she said, "When you hold resentment toward another, you are bound to that person by an emotional link that is stronger than steel. Forgiveness is the only way to dissolve that link and get free."

The biggest mistake people make when it comes to forgiveness is to believe that it is a favor one does for the one who has wronged them. It was Suzanne Somers who said it best when she said, "Forgiveness is a gift you give yourself."

Lewis B. Smedes said it this way: "To forgive is to set a prisoner free and discover that the prisoner was you." Alan Paton pointed out, "When deep injury is done us, we never recover until we forgive."

Another mistake people make when it comes to forgiveness is to believe that forgiveness is a sign of weakness and spine-lessness if you don't "stand up for yourself." Actually, as Mohandas Gandhi pointed out, "The weak can never forgive. Forgiveness is the attribute of the strong."

The refusal to forgive keeps one imprisoned in the past. Paul Boese put it this way: "Forgiveness does not change the past, but it does enlarge the future." Archbishop Desmund Tutu of South Africa said, "Without forgiveness, there is no future." Forgiveness is basically a choice to have a future over a past.

The biggest obstacle of all to forgiveness is the belief that the one who wrongs you needs to apologize, make amends and show evidence of change. While that is certainly part of justice, it is not essential.

Forgiveness is most powerful when it is unilateral and un-conditional. Unilateral and unconditional forgiveness is a sign of ultimate strength, because when you forgive unilaterally, you take charge of your situation and refuse to be someone else's victim any longer.

I have been a priest for 41 years. I can honestly say that the most spiritual experience of my life was not the day I was or-dained, not the day I said my first Mass, baptized my first baby, married my first couple, anointed my own mother before she died or presided at my first funeral. The most spiritual experi-ence of my life was the day I decided consciously to forgive and seek forgiveness. I finally realized that taking offense is just as toxic as giving offense.

July 21, 2011

The Real Test of Forgiveness

Love your enemies.
MATTHEW 5:44

As far as I know, I do not have a whole lot of enemies. I try to get along with most people. However, as much as I try, there always seem to be one or two people in my life who treat me like an enemy, though we have not had enough contact to have "words" or even to "make a scene."

Sometimes, they simply send me a vicious letter because I wrote something they did not like. Sometimes they are people who let me know they dislike me by snubbing me every time I run into them. If I try to speak, they simply look past me and walk away.

I used to think that if someone disliked me, it was always because there was something bad about me that I could not see. Lately, I have been trying to train myself to look behind their meanness and try to see where they are hurting, and if I can find the source, to do what I can to help heal that wound by filling the need behind it.

A couple of years ago, I noticed that one of my co-workers seemed to be going out of his way to ignore me. He seemed to resent my very presence. It bothered me immensely because I was trying to fit in and be a team player. My anger level began to rise, until one day I decided that he was so insecure about himself that he saw me as a threat to his favored place among the students.

Instead of being angry and defensive, I decided not to confront him directly, but to do what I could to make him feel important and valued. I went out of my way to affirm him in public and to send him notes of congratulations after his successful programs. It worked. He now treats me as a valued co-worker and even jokes with me occasionally.

Several years ago, as soon as I arrived at one of my parishes, one woman "took me on." She was obviously trying to get my goat. I remember saying to myself, "If I take the bait, this woman and I will be mortal enemies in no time."

I decided to "kill her with kindness," because I suspected that she was one of those people who had already decided that I would not like her and so she had decided not to like me first because her own sense of self-worth was so low. I kept up my program of affirming her and making over her whenever possible for the years I was there. Guess who cried hardest when I left?

Loving one's enemies is a basic tenet of Christianity – maybe the hardest tenet to live. One of the best ways to "love one's enemies" is to put oneself in their shoes, try to see where they are hurting and feed their need. It works.

June 14, 2007

Why Are People Mean?

He is so mean that no one can talk to him.
1 SAMUEL 25:17

As a follow up to last week's column and last summer's "debt debates," and in light of today's anniversary of our infamous 9-11 attack, I would like to say a few words about a growing phenomenon — "meanness."

As I noted last week, writing can actually be hazardous to one's health. While it is true that ninety-nine percent of the feedback I get (at least to my face) is very positive, I have gotten my share of pretty mean responses. The negative responses range from ridicule and outright attack to "bombs" wrapped in humor. Being a writer is a lot like being on the "Gong Show."

Here's how I handle caustic criticism. If I have never heard a positive comment from them, I tend to chalk it up to the fact that I have triggered some pain going on inside them. If they have been generous in affirming me for something in the past, then I tend to take to heart what they are saying and look for the problem residing in me.

There is a lot of meanness going around today — most of it much more serious than what I have reported above. Years ago, John Steinbeck may have summarized our world today when he said that we "admire kindness, generosity, openness, honesty, understanding and feeling, but we know that sharpness, greed, acquisitiveness, meanness, egotism and self-interest work."

Being nice is now associated with failure, while being mean is associated with success.

I don't know about you, but my first response to meanness is to be mean back! My second response is to take the poison in and let my wound get infected. My third and best response (when I am strong spiritually and emotionally) is to try to not take it in, but to keep it "out there" until I can understand it.

Why are people mean? Meanness seems to be an attempt at domination by people who believe that they have been hurt, that they have no power and that their pain may return again. It is a way for the mean person to try to diminish the power of the person he or she is being mean to and, therefore, gain that power. It's a rush, almost like a drug — "Look how miserable I can make this person."

The secret to diffusing the situation is to refuse to "bite" (or, as Jesus put it, "turn the other cheek"), thereby not granting the sought-after "payoff." This takes an incredible amount of self-confidence, self-discipline and spiritual maturity.

The question I like to ask myself when I feel attacked by mean people is, "What is the problem behind this problem?" I try to identify the hurting in the one being mean and try to heal it. If I cannot, I try to resolve to say nothing — what I call "not hitting the ball back over the net." When I do that, the game is usually over pretty quickly.

September 1, 2011

Magnanimity

If you love those who love you what right do you have to claim any credit? – MATTHEW 5:46

One of the most useful insights I have ever stumbled across was one from the Nazi concentration camp survivor, Victor Frankl, in his book, *Man's Search for Meaning*. He wrote these deeply meaningful and truly useful words: "Everything can be taken away from a man but one thing — the ability to choose one's attitude in any given set of circumstances."

We cannot always control what happens to us or around us, but we can choose how we want to respond. Things do not always work out. People divorce. Employees need to be fired. Children break our hearts. Friends let us down. Parents fail at parenting. In a world where revenge, vindictiveness, reciprocation, retribution and retaliation seem to be the most typical responses, we can train ourselves to respond differently.

Today, I would like to talk about the virtue of magnanimity, meaning to be generous in forgiving, eschewing resentment or revenge, and being unselfish and other-focused. The word comes from two Latin words: magna, meaning great, and animus, meaning soul or mind. Being magnanimous means being "big minded" or "great souled." It has nothing to do with who is right or who is wrong. It simply means to freely choose to be "noble" regardless of who is right and who is wrong.

It is really about "making a good ending" by choosing to be "big minded" or "great souled" regardless. Magnanimity is possible only for those who are not addicted to being right and who do not have a burning need to be faultless.

In life, we come face to face with unexpected circumstances, people who let us down and things that do not turn out the way we want them to be. Misunderstandings, human mistakes, bitter disappointments and shattered dreams are actually part of normal living. The more important thing to remember in those circumstances is that what happens is often not nearly as important as how we choose to react to what happens.

It takes magnanimity to go through a divorce without bitter vindictiveness and revenge. This is especially true when children are involved. In such cases, we might not be able to teach them about the permanence of marriage, but we can teach them about how to be civil, gracious and respectful with adversaries. It is as much of a gift to oneself as it is to the other, because it takes too much energy to carry a grudge.

It takes magnanimity to forgive an ungrateful or hurtful child and treat them well without being bitter, resentful, caustic and hostile. All the time and energy it takes to nurse wounds that we would as soon not heal is ultimately self-punishing anyway. It takes magnanimity to forgive a friend and make the first move toward reconciliation without needing to exact an apology. That is noble indeed. Taking the high road of humility is not a bad road to take for a friendship worth saving.

March 24, 2011

That's Funny!

There is a time to weep and a time to laugh.

ECCLESIASTES 3:4

At a time when nothing seems funny in the church anymore, I thought these stories might make you smile.

Cardinal Alfredo Ottaviani, a tenacious watchdog of orthodoxy, was a major defender of the status quo at the Second Vatican Council. One story from Vatican II days had him hopping into a Roman taxicab and exclaiming to the driver, "Take me to the Council!" His reputation solidly entrenched in people's minds, the driver headed for the city of Trent (the scene of a council 400 years before).

When Bishop Carroll Dozier became Bishop of Memphis, Tenn., in 1971, he soon scheduled a general absolution ceremony in a sports arena. Some 14,000 showed up. Rome did not approve of general absolution except for emergency circumstances, such as existed in battle areas during World War II. Bishop Dozier blamed Cardinal Spellman of New York when he was summoned to Rome to appear before the Congregation for Divine Worship and Discipline of the Sacraments to be reproved and directed not to repeat the ceremony.

When Bishop Dozier's plane circled New York in preparation for landing, an unchastened Bishop Dozier joshed to a friend, "I looked out the window, raised my right hand and absolved the whole city of New York – everyone, that is, except Cardinal Spellman!"

When Cardinal Sarto of Venice was elected Pope Pius X, he had pawned all his personal possessions to help the poor. When it came time for him to appear on the balcony overlooking St. Peter's Square after his election as pope, all he had was a cheap tin cross, because he had pawned his silver episcopal cross. Some were troubled, but not the new pope. "No one will notice. It looks quite like the real thing!"

Most people have heard Pope John XXIII's most famous joke. He was showing a visitor around the Vatican one day, and the visitor asked how many persons worked there. "About half," Pope John replied.

Cardinal Cushing of Boston was famous for his small regard for pomp and circumstance. At confirmation ceremonies, he would pace about and ask those to be confirmed questions from the catechism. He posed easy questions and glossed over blunders.

At one such ceremony, Cardinal Cushing came across Michael Cronin, son of Joe Cronin, then manager of the Boston Red Sox. "Who made the world?" Cardinal Cushing asked Michael. "God made the world," said Michael. "Who made the Red Sox?" Cardinal Cushing countered. "Tom Yawkey," declared the youth, citing the then-current owner of the Red Sox. Cardinal Cushing waited for the laughter to subside, then said: "You certainly know your catechism!"

Bishop Sheen, a great fund raiser for the missions, liked to tell the story of a young girl who was hugely successful raising money for the missions. Many of her customers returned three or four times. Her mother asked her where she was getting all the lemonade. The girl answered, "From the cocktail shaker you had in the icebox."

July 14, 2011

Only God Can See Into Our Hearts

If you pull up the weeds, you might uproot the wheat along with them. Let them grow together until the harvest. – MATTHEW 13

Religious fanatics have probably done more damage to religion than all the atheists, agnostics or public sinners put together. Blind as bats and cocksure, they claim to have perfect eyesight when it comes to good and evil, setting themselves up as judges, juries and executioners.

We are painfully familiar with fanatic Muslims who would fly planes into high-rise buildings as a way to rid the world of "degenerate western influences" and Puritans who would burn "witches" at the stake to keep the church "pure."

In our own church, fanatics had a heyday in what we know as the "Inquisition," a misguided effort to rid the church of heresy, error and sin that used some of the most vicious, cruel, inhuman and unchristian methods imaginable. Many good and holy, even saintly, people were brutally killed by these awful people, all in the name of God, of course. Jesus warns us to beware of such overzealous religious weed-eaters.

In this parable, Jesus tells us that in his kingdom here on earth, the good and the bad exist alongside one another, and nobody but God can really tell the difference. To make his point, he turns to farming for a parable. He tells the story of a farmer who plants good seed, only to find out that, as it sprouts, weeds appear right there with it. God is that farmer.

One day, the farmer's hired hands (that's us) report the presence of weeds growing among the wheat and offer to crank up their big "weed-eaters" and go to work on them. The farmer gives them a quick and firm, "No! Don't you dare! Leave them alone! Let them grow together 'til the harvest! It's too early now because you can t tell one from the other! Wait 'til harvest time!"

The point of the parable is that, unlike human beings who tend to judge quickly, God is lenient and patient. The parable clearly reflects Jesus own experience of condemnation by religious people for associating with social outcasts. The message to us is this: Yes, good and evil exist side by side in the church and in the world, but beware of overzealous, fanatic "weed-eaters" who want to clean things up for God. More times than not, they do more harm than good.

It is important to remember that Jesus is not saying the difference between good and evil is not important. He is obviously for good and against evil, but the point he is making here is simply this: As the Christian community moves through history, it is composed of good and bad people. But we cannot always be sure who is who. The community has a right to teach principles, but ultimately it is God's business to make the separation, because "people see externals, but only God can see into hearts."

November 21, 2002

The Well of Satisfaction

Whoever drinks the water I shall give will never thirst.
JOHN 4:14

So far this Lent Jesus has invited us to conversion of life by going to the desert for insight and to the mountain for perspective. This Sunday he invites us to go to his well for true satisfaction.

The prophet Haggai, about 520 years before Christ, described our culture quite well when he wrote, "You have sown much, but have brought in little; you have eaten, but have not been satisfied; you have drunk, but not been exhilarated; have clothed yourselves, but not been warmed; and you have earned wages for a bag with holes in it."

It has been suggested that our consumer culture has spawned a new climate of restlessness. The experts call it "churn," using the word to describe our short attention span and "what's next" attitude. This restlessness is seen in the lust for endless distractions and amusements that consume us.

This restlessness is being fed, some believe, by the over-stimulation and excessive exposure to violent movies, fast-paced videos, computers and cell phones, loud and hard-wired music, and over-scheduling. All these together exacerbate agitation, restlessness and hyperactivity.

What the world seems to be craving right now is what Jesus called "rest for your souls." He said, "Come to me, all who labor and are heavy laden, and I will give you rest. Take my yoke upon you and learn from me, for I am gentle and lowly in heart, and you will find rest for your souls."

In this Sunday's gospel, the woman Jesus meets at the well is tired, tired to the bone. She is tired of being thirsty and having to carry water. She is tired of trying to find a satisfying relationship. She is tired of being rejected by others. At the well, she meets Jesus and pours out her heart to him, and he, in turn, gives her "living water" and "rest for her soul."

All of us have a void in our lives. Some of us strive our whole lives to gain things, to gain stature, to get to the top of the ladder, to gain fame, to find the perfect relationship and much more, in a frantic effort to fill that void. The fact of the matter is we will never fill that void with "things" or "stuff," because that void was put there for a specific purpose.

What is the purpose of that void? It is the place where God belongs! St. Augustine of Hippo described it best when he said, "You have made us for yourself, O Lord, and our heart is restless until it finds its rest in you!"

The best meditation for this third Sunday of Lent could be Francis Thompson's "The Hound of Heaven":

> "I fled him, down the nights and down the days; I fled him, down the arches of the years; I fled him, down the labyrinthine ways of my own mind; and in the midst of tears I hid from him."

March 8, 2012

Spiritual Power

The whole city was shaken when Jesus entered Jerusalem.
MATTHEW 21:1-11

I am convinced that many Catholics think the first Palm Sunday was like some kind of Pegasus Parade, with the streets lined on each side with happy, cheering crowds and Jesus and his donkey serving as the central float. Nothing could be further from the truth! This was no nice parade.

Things were crowded and tense in Jerusalem when Jesus arrived for the Passover in 32 A.D. Jesus was considered a popular religious and political revolutionary. The religious establishment was jealous of his popularity among the common folk. They feared he wanted to revolutionize their old-time religion.

Jesus had only recently charged through the Temple precincts, overturning the money changers, accusing the religious establishment of corrupting the Jewish religion and turning it into a financial racket. The political establishment was paranoid that his arrival could trigger a riot. They feared he wanted to be king. Tensions had reached a boiling point. The whole city was on edge.

Palm waving and the throwing of coats on the road were not just some spontaneous gestures of welcome. These two actions had serious political overtones. They were synonymous with flag waving. People threw their coats on the road when a new king arrived to ascend his throne, and palm waving was a symbol of Jewish nationalism.

Even though the people had tried to make Jesus a king in hopes that he would be the one to throw the hated Romans out of their land, Jesus had said "no" on more than one occasion to being the political revolutionary they wanted.

With the crowds in that frame of mind, no wonder the Roman authorities were nervous that day. The text says "… the whole city was shaken when Jesus entered Jerusalem."

Jesus himself knew that his arrival in Jerusalem under those circumstances smacked of a showdown. In response to the people's misguided reception of him as some kind of religious and political revolutionary, Jesus came into the city, not in a chariot pulled by white horses, but on the back of a jackass.

By choosing that kind of animal, the animal of the poor, Jesus made the statement that he did not come with political power, but with spiritual power. The people just didn't want to hear it. They wanted a powerful Jewish king, and so this symbol of humility simply went over their heads. They wanted to be freed from oppressive religious and political leadership, and they wanted it now.

Palm Sunday has a lot to teach the church, even today. My friends, our power is not to be found in political power. Turning to political power is the clearest sign that we have failed to inspire a conversion of heart.

Our power is even more powerful than political power. In fact, we have been most weak spiritually when we have been most aligned with political power. We have been most powerful when we have been humble and honest in the eyes of the world.

March 29, 2012

Doubt Is Not the Opposite of Faith

When the eleven disciples saw Jesus, they worshipped, even as they doubted. – MATTHEW 28

"They worshipped Jesus even when they doubted." That's pretty much the opposite of what we do. When we doubt, we tend to quit worshipping. We assume that worshipping is only for believers.

The first thing many people assume about faith is that doubt is the opposite of faith. Not true. Honest doubt is not the opposite of faith. Honest doubt is actually an integral part of faith.

"They worshipped, even as they doubted." More important than whether doubt is part of faith is what to do about doubt. Many, when they doubt, remove themselves from worship. They say to themselves, "It is hypocritical for me to pretend to believe when I really don't believe. When I start believing, when my faith is strong, then it will make sense for me to start praying and worshipping."

That may sound good, even reasonable, but that's not how it works. As the disciples teach us, what really works is for us to "pray through" our doubt, to worship until we believe.

"They worshipped, even as they doubted." This may be yet another version of the great truth: "Fake it till you make it." Even though Alcoholics Anonymous made that idea famous, it actually goes back to the ancient Roman poet, Ovid, who said,

"Pretend to be what is not, and then you'll become in truth what you are pretending to be." The great philosopher William James put it this way, "Act as if, and the mind will produce your desire."

The idea is, if you take something that feels impossible, or at least completely unnatural, and pretend that it is the easiest, most natural thing in the world for you to be doing, eventually it will become as easy as you're pretending it to be.

I practice this often in my own life. I grew up pretty much crippled by bashfulness. Bashful people find it painful to be in public situations. To cope, they try to avoid public situations as much as possible. This is a sure way to keep bashfulness going. The solution is to get out in public and fake confidence. You cannot think your way out of bashfulness; you have to act your way out.

When I was sent to southeastern Kentucky as a newly ordained priest, I decided to "fake it till I made it." Since I did not get what I wanted – which was not to be sent to southeastern Kentucky – I decided to pretend to want what I got until I was able to really want what I got. By acting as if it was a great assignment, it became a great assignment.

My friends, all of us have a good measure of doubt, even as we believe. The secret to a stronger faith is to act as if we have a strong faith until our faith is strengthened, to worship until we want to worship. Even believers sometimes have to "fake it 'til they make it."

June 2, 2005

The Self-Righteous

Your mother and your brothers and sisters are outside looking for you. – MARK 3

Unlike the evangelists who came after him, the writer of Mark's Gospel has an uncanny way of laying things out for you, unvarnished. As respect and reverence for the apostles rose in the early church, we find some of the stories in his Gospel "cleaned up" in the Gospels that came later.

We see this in the story about the ambitions of James and John. Mark says that the request for the best seats in Jesus' new kingdom came out of the mouths of James and John. When Matthew tells the same story later, this tacky request comes out of the mouth of their mother. It's an old, and often useful, trick in ministry – to blame women.

We see this again in today's story about the family of Jesus showing up to see him. Both Matthew and Luke record the story, but with one big difference. Mark and Matthew both tell us that Jesus' family showed up looking for a chance to speak with him, but only Mark tells us why they wanted to see Jesus.

In a few verses proceeding today's reading, we are told that his family "set out to seize Jesus because they said he was out of his mind." They were convinced that he had "lost it," and they wanted to take him home for his own good.

Ever since Adam and Eve there has been a tendency among humans to believe that they know better than God himself what needs to be done. In prayer, instead of asking God to change us so that we will do his will, we often attempt to use prayer as a way to bribe God to do our will. It is like the funny prayer I saw recently that says, "Use me Lord! Use me! Use me in some advisory capacity."

One warning to those of you who are clergy or pastoral workers. There have been many before us who started off speaking about God, but gradually moved toward speaking for God. After that, it is a short step to speaking as if you are God. From there, it is easy to think that even God is "out of his mind" and needs our advice.

Beware of preachers and politicians who are more than willing to clean up things for God. Ann Coulter says about the Middle East, "We ought to invade their countries, kill their leaders and convert them to Christianity." Jerry Falwell says, "The idea that religion and politics don't mix was invented by the devil to keep Christians from running their own country." Pat Robertson says that Ariel Sharon's stroke was inflicted by God as punishment. Jimmy Swaggart says, "If I don't return to the pulpit this weekend, millions of people will go to hell."

There may be no people more dangerous than the self-righteous who speak for God, because sooner or later they begin to believe they are God.

March 23, 2006

Possibility

No one pours new wine into old wineskins. New wine is poured into fresh wineskins. – MARK 2

One of my heroes is Philo T. Farnsworth. I have a framed quote of his hanging on a very visible wall in my house. It says, "Impossible things just take a little longer."

If you don't recognize his name, you should. He is credited with inventing television. He believed that with an open mind anything was possible. Look how far television, once labeled "impossible," has come.

The reason Philo T. Farnsworth is a hero of mine is that I, too, believe that more things are possible than we can ever imagine. The realization of the impossible begins with an open mind. When I have consciously and deliberately kept my mind open, I have seen this dynamic unfold more times than I can count.

Negative thinking kills the possible. Here are a couple of examples from real life.

A shoe factory once sent two marketing scouts to a region of Africa to study the prospects for expanding the shoe business. One sent back a telegram that said, "Situation hopeless. No one wears shoes." The other sent back a telegram saying, "Great business opportunity. They have no shoes."

Thomas Watson, chairman of IBM, responded negatively to the idea of investing in computers in 1943 by saying, "I think there is a world market for maybe five computers." As late as

1977, Ken Olson, president, chairman and founder of Digital Equipment Corporation said, "There is no reason anyone would want a computer in his home."

As a child, if I had not decided to reject it, I would have been a victim of this kind of negative thinking. Several significant adults in my life told me that I had no chance at all of making it through the seminary. I was even called a "hopeless case" by one seminary rector.

Because of these experiences, I stay in a mild state of irritation at our church when it seems unable to take advantage of the many opportunities staring it in the face even now. No wonder we have a vocation crisis. No wonder we are closing parishes. We are hopelessly mired in downward spiraling talk about both issues. Where are the can-do people who can see an alternative to our hopeless resignation?

Jesus tells us that God needs an open mind, a "new wineskin," to do his work of making all things new. Mary understood this when she said "yes" to God. She knew that when an open mind cooperates with God, then "all things are possible."

I pray for this kind of mind and heart. My prayer for this kind of mind and heart can be summed up in the words of Soren Kierkegaard when he said, "If I were to wish for anything I should not wish for wealth and power, but for the passionate sense of what can be, for the eye, which, ever young and ardent, sees the possible."

Faith can move mountains.

April 6, 2006

Miracles

All who touched the tassel of his robe were restored to health. – MARK 6:56

When you get old like I am, you realize that you have a few books on your shelf that were the source of breakthroughs in understanding. Those books are usually not among those that are recognized as "great" by anybody else but yourself. They may have brought you only one memorable insight, but that insight was eye-opening.

Such is the case with two books by Father Louis Evely. With one, I had a great breakthrough in my understanding of the purpose of prayer and with the other in my understanding of faith healing.

Father Evely makes the case that the phenomenon known as a "miracle" is simply the manifestation of the natural world not yet understood. A "miracle," he says, does not happen from the outside in but from the inside out. Christ did not tell those he cured, "My power has cured you." Instead, he said, "Your faith has cured you."

In fact, Mark (6:5) reports that "Jesus could work no miracle there because of people's lack of faith." It was not touching the holy tassel that cured the people in the Gospel that day; it was the faith of those who touched his tassel that triggered their cures!

What about the miracles that have been recorded at places like Lourdes? Well, there have been miracles at every shrine of every religion, and most of these have been miracles of healing.

Father Evely notes that the sole characteristic of a miraculous cure is the extraordinary acceleration of the natural healing process. That which cannot be healed by a natural process is not susceptible to a miraculous cure; an amputated leg or arm, for example, has never been regrown miraculously — not even a finger. So it seems that such acceleration of the natural processes of healing can be triggered by faith.

It's not the sacred stone, the holy relic, the water from a mysterious water source or even the tassel of Jesus' cloak that causes the healing, but the intensity of faith of those who believe that triggers their extraordinarily rapid healing processes. As Jesus said to another tassel-touching believer, a woman with a hemorrhage, "It is your faith that saved you."

I believe in the power of faith to work miracles. In almost every assignment I have ever had, I have had to override the negative advice I was given by my predecessors. I was advised not to get my hopes up because "nothing could be done because this or that situation was hopeless." By choosing to believe in amazing possibilities, I have been amazed at the results in all those assignments.

Even doctors will tell you that people have mysteriously gotten well when they are able to believe that getting well is possible, while they have mysteriously lost patients who gave up on their treatment programs. Even Henry Ford said, "Those who believe they can and those who think they can't are both right."

March 8, 2007

When Bad Things Happen to Good People

We accept good things from God. Should we not then accept the bad? – JOB 2:10

Why do good people have to suffer through things like the ravages of cancer and its treatments, only to die?

I have been asked various versions of this question, as well as heard versions of attempted answers, throughout my almost 38 years of priesthood. My answer is simple. I haven't the foggiest idea, and neither does anyone else. The bottom line is, nobody really knows, including those of good will who try to come up with something comforting to say.

It is better, I think, to just sit with the mystery. Anything else comes across as irritatingly trite or nauseatingly sentimental.

The biblical story of Job makes this very point. One day, God and the devil discuss the Job family. Even God brags about how good and faithful the Job family has been. The devil listens to all God has to say about them, but then says to God, "Sure! Who wouldn't love you if they had it as good the Job family has it? It's easy to believe when things are going well, but just start taking a few things away from them and then you'll see just how faithful they are."

In this little play, God allows Satan to start taking things away to test Job's fidelity. First, Job loses his money. Next, he loses his children in a freak accident. Finally, Job loses his health. Through all this, the last line of our reading tells us that

Job never curses God, even though his wife suggests it. He neither questions God nor does anything sinful.

The story ends without a convincing reason being given for Job's suffering. However, because Job remained faithful in the absence of answers, God makes the latter part of Job's life even better than the first!

When we are faced with the mystery of suffering and death, we have no real answers. However, we do have a choice about how we want to respond. We can be bitter about what we lost, or we can be grateful for what we had. Entitlement leads us into bitterness. Gratitude leads us into peaceful acceptance. When we feel entitled, gratitude is impossible.

Feelings of entitlement make us believe that life owes us something, and when it is taken away, we feel angry, resentful, cheated and frustrated. However, in reality, entitlement is an illusion. With life being as it is, entitlement is a perfect setup for disappointment because it is based on a lie to begin with. We are owed nothing in this life, and the truth of the matter is, everything is a gift. We deserve nothing, and everything is on loan — even our loved ones.

On the other hand, if we believe that life and everything in it is a gift, we can experience painful losses, even death, in a radically different way. Instead of being bitter about what we lost, we can become grateful for what we had.

March 13, 2008

Walking with God

Faith is the realization of what is hoped for and the evidence of things not seen. – HEBREWS 11:1

I have been at this "priest thing" almost all of my life. I have never really wanted to be anything else. I first felt "called" when I was seven years old, and I started seminary at age 14. I was ordained at 26.

I have been a priest now for 34 years. Last year, for the first time in my life, I actually thought about quitting. I was so angry, disappointed, embarrassed and disillusioned that I thought about throwing in the towel, moving out of state and finding a job that had nothing to do with God, the church or priesthood. I wanted to quit, but I didn't. I can't.

The question I kept coming back to was this one: "Where is my faith placed?" Is my faith in priests? No! Is it in bishops? No! Is it in the pope? No! They are merely "earthenware jars." They hold the "treasure," but they are not the "treasure." Is it in organized religion? No! Organized religion has and will always be in need of reform.

I finally came to this conclusion: to leave would be to turn my back on God. How could I turn my back on the God who called me to be a priest simply because the going is rough? How could I go off and leave my "faith family" in its time of need?

After exploring the possibility of leaving, wallowing in my depression and wrestling with the question of faith, I finally came to the realization that if I have faith at all, then this is the time to prove it — by staying and remaining faithful.

Do you have faith? No, I don't mean do you believe that this or that Bible story happened or this or that church doctrine to be true. I mean, do you really trust God? Can you keep walking with God, even when you can't see where you are going, even when your most precious things, relationships and assumptions are taken away from you?

I am amazed at people who say they have "lost their faith" when a church is renovated, an altar rail is removed, a Mass time is changed, a school is closed or a church member disappoints them. If faith only holds up when things are going fine, when the world is the way we like it, when we are blessed with all that life has to offer, when every church member is perfect, then it is not faith.

Is your faith being tested? Here is how you will know if you have passed the test. If we can go on loving and trusting God after we hear the diagnosis of cancer, after our house burns down, after we lose our job, after our spouse dies and after our friends abandon us – after we lose everything we can lose – then we can say we have faith.

September 9, 2004

Giving God Our All

You shall love God with all your
heart, soul, mind and strength.
MARK 12

Love God with all my heart, soul, mind and strength? You mean I am supposed to put God in the very center and make God the most important consideration in my life? Most of us, to be honest, can't say that God is that important to us.

I would love to be able to say that God is always at the center my life, but sadly, I put myself and other things ahead of God sometimes. Some days I do better than others, but thankfully, God is very patient with me and loves me anyway. I have always taken comfort in knowing that my best is good enough for God.

Today, I want to say a few more words about taking God seriously. None of us will ever measure up completely to the Great Commandment – the one that summarizes all other commandments – but this is the brass ring for which we all reach. To take God seriously, to seek to love him with all we have, there are things we must do.

• We must want what God wants. To want what God wants means we have to understand the Scriptures, listen to the Spirit within us and stay consciously connected to God through prayer.

• We must remember who we are. We are holy. We are holy not because of what we have done, but because we are "created in the image and likeness of God," and, through our baptism, we are adopted children of God. We must accept our holiness, neither exaggerating nor denying who we really are.

• We must want to live by the same values Jesus lived by: having a loving kindness toward all, especially the most weak and vulnerable, even our enemies; striving to do God's will no matter the consequences; using Jesus' own life as a pattern for our own.

• We must be in command of ourselves, have a handle on our addictions and our passions, so that we can go in the way that God wants us to go. We must constantly question our own motives, making sure that we not only do the right thing, but also do it for the right reason.

• We must never give in to hopelessness, whether it is about the future or about other people. We know the war against evil has already been won, even though we may continue to lose many painful battles. God's kingdom will come, and nothing we do, not even the gates of hell, can stop it.

• Regardless of our failures, loving God with our whole heart, soul, mind and strength is something we should strive for, even though it is something we will never accomplish completely. God wants a relationship with us, even if it is rocky and imperfect.

We are challenged to get serious about God, not in some loud, noisy and superficial way, but in a long haul and to the core-of-one's-being kind of way.

May 24, 2007

Talk to Yourself

Then I shall say to myself, "You have so many good things stored up for years to come. Rest, eat, drink, be merry!"
— LUKE 12:19

There is an old Jackson Browne song, "Take It Easy," that contains a line that has always stuck in my mind: "Don't let the sound of your own wheels make you crazy." What he is referring to, of course, is that incessant inner dialogue that most of us have going on in our heads throughout the day.

Even though mind-chatter can be positive, for many of us it is, more often than not, negative. Though we work hard to improve our situations, our negative thinking keeps sabotaging our work, leaving us wondering why there seems to be no progress.

Are you aware of your inner dialogue? Some say that how much fulfillment you get in your life is directly proportional to the quality of your inner dialogue. Henry Ford was right when he said, "Those who think they can, and those who think they can't, are both right."

As a young man, I was told by several adults that I "could not do anything right" and "would never amount to anything." That wasn't helpful, but the bigger problem was that I had started believing them and feeding myself similar messages. It was only when I started feeding myself positive messages that I began to come into my own.

A positive experience of this dynamic came my way around 1983. More and more people were telling me that I should publish my homilies. I always had an excuse. I did not have time. I did not have a publisher. The real problem was that I was still telling myself that I was not good enough to be a writer.

As my excuses were being shot down, it became clear to me one day that I needed to change my own self-sabotaging internal dialogue. I repeated encouraging messages to myself, daily, for two years until one day an editor from a publishing company mysteriously showed up. With 13 books in print, I can now say that I am a writer.

This dynamic works for our good as well as our undoing, especially if we constantly feed ourselves negative messages. Victims of spouse abuse never make it out of their abuse as long as they think they don't deserve anything better. It is only when they are able to say, "I deserve to be treated with respect," and say it enough that they start believing it, that their freedom can be achieved.

Affirmations, litanies, mantras and prayers such as the "Jesus Prayer" have this in common: they are all a few words, repeated over and over again at regular intervals, until God opens the subconscious mind to accept them and then begins to go to work to bring them about. God doesn't need to be persuaded to give, but the human heart often needs to be persuaded to receive.

How have you been talking to yourself lately? Have you been critical or encouraging?

April 30, 2009

Creating Yourself

You have taken off the old self and put on the new self,
which is being renewed. – COLOSSIANS 3:9,10

With book 16 at the press, I have started a 17th! The one I
am working on now is another one for priests, entitled *Molding
Yourself Into the Priest You Are Called to Be: Self-Formation
in Priestly Formation.* I got the idea from Blessed Pope John
Paul II: "All formation, priestly formation included, is ultimately self-formation."

I would like to share one of those principles, because I
think it applies to more than priests. I believe that this principle applies to all of us. We have more power to create the
selves we want to be than we know.

As you look at your own life, which of the following state-
ments is more true?

"Life is something that happens to you, and all you
can do is make the most of it."

"Life is not about finding yourself; life is about creating yourself."

"Do you feel more like a passenger in someone else's
car or the driver behind the wheel of your own?"

"Do you feel you have the bull by the horns or that
you are being dragged by it?"

I do believe that some people have had more advantages,
opportunities and luck than others, but I also believe that we

have more power than we know to be more than we are, regardless of advantages, opportunities or luck. How else can we account for those who have overcome great obstacles to rise to great heights and those who have crashed and burned from the heights of great advantage, opportunity and luck?

We are more powerful than we know in creating the lives we want, as long as we get over our belief in magic, as long as we quit clinging conveniently to a sense of victimhood and as long as we stand up to our own lazy cowardice. Even when we have lost everything, even when we are dying from a terminal illness, we are still powerful, because we can always choose how we want to respond to it.

Self-creation takes courage, and because it takes courage, we often sabotage our own success because it makes life less difficult, less risky, less scary and less threatening.

Often we are held back by the beliefs about ourselves that we have come to accept or have absorbed from others. With low self-esteem, we avoid being powerful, and we unconsciously choose to be helpless. We withdraw from the simplest demands in a task, as well as from life's opportunities.

Feeling powerless, we want to be taken care of. We look for strong people to lean on and upon whom we can be dependent. We become "feverish little clods of grievances and ailments, complaining that the world will not get together to make us happy." We are afraid to admit that much of what we hate about our lives is the result of a long series of lazy choices over a lifetime.

June 30, 2011

May God's Love Shine Through for You

> Upon those who dwelt in the land of gloom
> a light has shone.
> ISAIAH 9:1

When I started writing this column more than two years ago, I chose the title "An Encouraging Word" because I wanted to offer a little hope to those who were struggling, especially those who found themselves struggling with the fallout of the "sexual abuse scandal" that exploded from secrecy into broad daylight.

If the truth be known, the writing itself gave me a way to work through my own depression and keep myself hopeful. The fact that it has helped others has been icing on the cake.

In this year's Christmas column, my third, I want to offer "an encouraging word" to those who dread the holidays because of sickness, sadness or loss. Like many priests with whom people share their pain, I am very aware that Christmas is not "jingle bells all the way" for everybody out there.

First, I would like to send "an encouraging word" to those who live alone, especially the elderly who have outlived most of their families and friends. As a priest, I have known what it is like to go back to an empty house or apartment alone, after Mass, when families go home together. I remember more than one Christmas when I went to bed just so I wouldn't have to feel the loneliness.

Second, I would like to send "an encouraging word" to those of you who are dealing with the uncertainty and pain of serious health problems, either personally, in your family or among your close friends. I know several people who are facing cancer, Alzheimer's or other chronic diseases. These things affect not just those who have them, but everyone around them. It is a time of testing: of one's patience, faith and even resources.

Third, I would like to send "an encouraging word" to those who have lost loved ones this year. Even though my mother died 28 years ago, I still get choked up at midnight Mass when I pause "to remember those who have gone before us." Those of you who have lost spouses, children, siblings or close friends this year, especially under tragic situations, will find this Christmas especially painful.

Last, I would like to send "an encouraging word" to the man who writes me from prison, the young woman who is grieving over the loss of a relationship, the children of addicted parents or struggling, divorced, single parents.

That first Christmas was certainly a day of promise, but it was also a day of pain. Mary and Joseph were away from home. Jesus was born in a barn. Herod was out to kill the newborn Jesus.

But, in spite of it all and behind all the details, the incredible love God has for us has shone through. So, no matter what you are facing this Christmas, may the incredible love God has for you shine through. May you know it. May you feel it.

December 23, 2004

QUOTES
BY THEME

A collection of the memorable and thought-provoking quotes cited in *An Encouraging Word*

AFFIRMATION

Nine-tenths of education is encouragement.
ANATOLE FRANCE

It does no harm once in a while to acknowledge that the whole country isn't in flames, that there are people in this country besides politicians, entertainers and criminals.
CHARLES KURALT

Those who are lifting the world upward and onward are those who encourage more than criticize.
ELIZABETH HARRISON

Let us stop thinking so much about punishing, criticizing and improving others. Instead, let us rather raise ourselves that much higher. Let us color our own example with ever more vividness.
FRIEDRICH NIETZSCHE

The meanest, most contemptible kind of praise is that which first speaks well of a man, and then qualifies it with a 'but.'
HENRY WARD BEECHER

You need to be aware of what others are doing, applaud their efforts, acknowledge their successes and encourage them in their pursuits. When we all help one another, everybody wins.
JIM STOVAL

Judicious praise is to children what the sun is to flowers.
UNKNOWN

AGING

We grow gray in spirit long before we grow gray in our hair.
CHARLES LAMB

Youth is a gift of nature, but age is a work of art.
GARSON KANIN

Old age is like flying through a storm.
Once you're aboard, there's nothing you can do.
GOLDA MEIR

Age is opportunity no less than youth itself,
though in another dress.
HENRY WADSWORTH LONGFELLOW

A man is not old until regrets take the place of dreams.
JOHN BARRYMORE

At 20 we worry about what others think of us; at 40
we don't care about what others think of us; at 60 we
discover they haven't been thinking about us at all.
MALCOLM FORBES

Age is an issue of mind over matter.
If you don't mind, it doesn't matter.
MARK TWAIN

ATTITUDE

If you don't think every day is a good day,
just try missing one.
CAVETT ROBERT

Happiness is an inside job.
DR. BERNIE SIEGEL

Believe that you will succeed ... believe it firmly and you will do what is necessary to bring it to success.
DALE CARNEGIE

People with goals succeed because they know where they are going ... it's as simple as that.
EARL NIGHTINGALE

Men are not prisoners of fate,
but only prisoners of their own minds.
FRANKLIN D. ROOSEVELT

The "Knots Prayer"
Dear God, please untie the knots that are in my
mind, my heart and my life.
Remove the have nots, the can nots and the do nots
that I have in my mind.
Erase the will nots, may nots, might nots that may
find a home in my heart.
Release me from the could nots, would nots and
should nots that obstruct my life.
And most of all, dear God, I ask that you remove
from my mind, my heart and my life all of the "am
nots" that I have allowed to hold me back, especially
the thought that I am not good enough.
Amen!

Those who think they can and those
who think they can't are both right.
HENRY FORD

A happy person is not a person in a certain set of circumstances, but rather a person with a certain set of attitudes.
HUGH DOWNS

What we see depends mainly on what we look for.
JOHN LUBBOCK

If you keep saying things are going to be bad,
you have a good chance of becoming a prophet.
ISAAC BASHEVIS SINGER

By believing passionately in that which does exist,
we create it. That which is nonexistent has not been
sufficiently desired.
NIKOS KAZANTZAKIS

You hear people complaining about this present day
and age because things were so much better in former times. I wonder what would happen if they
could be taken back to the days of their ancestors —
would we not still hear them complaining? You may
think past ages were good, but it is only because you
are not living in them.
ST. AUGUSTINE

I cannot change the direction of the wind,
but I can adjust my sails.
UNKNOWN

It ain't what they call you, it's what you answer to!
W. C. FIELDS

The greatest discovery of my generation is that a
human being can alter his life by altering his attitudes.
WILLIAM JAMES

CHANGE

All things that resist change are changed by that resistance
in ways undesired and undesirable.
GARRY WILLIS

The most fatal illusion is the settled point of view.
BROOKS ATKINSON

To get what you want, stop doing what isn't working.
DENNIS WEAVER

When you change the way you look at things,
the things you look at change.
DR. WAYNE DYER

The only constant in life is change.
FRANCOIS DE LA ROCHEFOUCALD

The interval between the decay of the old and the
formation and establishment of the new constitutes a
period of transaction which must always necessarily
be one of uncertainty, confusion, error, and wild and
fierce fanaticism.
JOHN C. CALHOUN - *VP UNDER JOHN QUINCY ADAMS*

...on facing transitions in one's life...
It's like being between trapezes. It's like Linus when
his blanket is in the dryer. There's nothing to hang onto."
MARILYN FERGUSON

You can judge your age by the amount of pain you feel
when you come into contact with a new idea.
PEARL BUCK

Tradition is creative. Always original, it always opens out to new horizons for an old journey. Those who are not humble hate their past and push it out of sight, just as they cut down the growing and green things that spring up inexhaustibly even in the present.
THOMAS MERTON

My life changed once things changed in me.
TYLER PERRY

Nothing gets better by leaving it alone.
WINSTON CHURCHILL

COURAGE

God will not have his work made manifest by cowards.
RALPH WALDO EMERSON

Courage is being scared to death, but saddling up anyway.
JOHN WAYNE

For love was offered me and I shrank from its disillusionment; sorrow knocked at my door, but I was afraid; ambition called me, but I dreaded the chance. Yet all the while I hungered for meaning in my life. And now I know that we must lift the sail and catch the winds of destiny wherever they drive the boat. To put meaning in one's life may end in madness, but life without meaning is the torture of restlessness and vague desire — it is a boat longing for the sea and yet afraid.
EDGAR LEE MASTERS - FROM *GEORGE GRAY*

People in mourning have to come to grips with death before they can live again. Mourning can go on for years and years. It doesn't end after a year; that's a false fantasy. It usually ends when people realize that they can live again, that they can concentrate their energies on their lives as a whole, and not on their hurt, and guilt and pain.

ELIZABETH KUBLER-ROSS

All that is necessary for the triumph of evil
is for enough good people to do nothing.

EDMUND BURKE

Christianity has not been tried and found wanting;
it has been found difficult and not tried.

G. K. CHESTERTON

Only those who risk going too far
can possibly find out how far they can go.

T.S. ELIOT

Faint not nor fear, but go out to the storm and the action, trusting in God whose commandment you faithfully follow; freedom, exultant, will welcome your spirit with joy.

DIETRICH BONHOEFFER
GERMAN LUTHERAN PASTOR, THEOLOGIAN, DISSIDENT ANTI-NAZI

The bravest thing you can do when you are not brave
is to profess courage and act accordingly.

CORA HARRIS

May you not forget the infinite possibilities
that are born of faith.

MOTHER TERESA

It is not the critic who counts: not the man who points out how the strong man stumbles, or where the doer of deeds could have done them better. The credit belongs to the man who is actually in the arena, whose face is marred by dust and sweat and blood: who strives valiantly, who errs, and comes up short again and again, because there is no effort without error or shortcoming; but who does actually strive to do the deeds; who knows the great enthusiasms, the great devotions; who spends himself in a worthy cause; who at best knows in the end the triumph of high achievement, and who at worst, if he fails, at least fails while daring greatly, so that his place shall never be with those cold and timid souls who know neither victory nor defeat.

THEODORE ROOSEVELT

You have to decide what your highest priorities are and have the courage to say no to other things. And the way to do that is by having a bigger yes burning inside you.

STEVEN COVEY

FAITH

I like your Christ. I do not like your Christians. Your Christians are so unlike your Christ.

GHANDI

Preach the Gospel at all times. Use words if necessary!

ST. FRANCIS OF ASSISI

It's time Christians were judged more by their likeness to Christ than their notions of Christ.

WILLIAM PENN

We think if we can dispense adequate information, people will be convinced that Jesus is the way, the truth and the life and turn to him. Those methods don't work anymore. I'm not sure they ever did. People aren't looking for information about God. They want to experience God himself. Information leaves them bored, uninterested. Experience, especially the ultimate experience any human being can ever have, leaves them breathless. And that is what we have to offer.

MARK TABB

FEAR

It's a dangerous business, Frodo, going out your door.

BILBO - TO FRODO IN *FELLOWSHIP OF THE RINGS*

It seems the necessary thing to do is not to fear mistakes, to plunge in, to do the best that one can, hoping to learn enough from blunders to correct them eventually.

ABRAHAM MASLOW

In order to succeed, your desire for success should be greater than your fear of failure.

BILL COSBY

The greatest mistake we make is living in constant fear that we will make one.

JOHN C. MAXWELL

A fear of the unknown keeps a lot of people from leaving bad situations.

KATHIE LEE GIFFORD

A boo is louder than a cheer. If you have ten people cheering and one person booing, all you hear is the booing.

LANCE ARMSTRONG

Our deepest fear is not that we are inadequate. Our deepest fear is that we are powerful beyond measure. It is our light, not our darkness, that most frightens us.

MARIANNE WILLIAMSON

FORGIVENESS

When deep injury is done us,
we never recover until we forgive.

ALAN PATON

Without forgiveness, there is no future.

DESMOND TUTU

People can be deeply hurt for life by a casual, flippant wisecrack or inspired forever by a genuine gesture of compassion and kindness.

BISHOP RICHARD SKLBA

The weak can never forgive.
Forgiveness is the attribute of the strong.

GANDHI

People shouldn't worry about their status before God at the moment of death. I don't think God judges us at our weakest moments, but at our strongest moment.

J. MOLTMANN

Forgiveness is a gift you give yourself.

SUZANNE SOMERS

If you look closely enough, you will realize
that he is doing the best he can.

KATHRYN HEPBURN TO HER DAUGHTER PLAYED BY JANE FONDA
IN *ON GOLDEN POND*, WHEN SHE WAS TERRIBLY FRUSTRATED
WITH HER AGGRAVATING, OLD FATHER.

Taking offense is just as destructive as giving offense.

KEN KEYES

To forgive is to set a prisoner free and
discover that the prisoner was you.

LEWIS B. SMEDES

I dreamed Death came the other night and Heaven's
gate swung wide.
With kindly grace an angel ushered me inside.
And there to my astonishment stood folks I'd known
on earth,
Some I'd judged and labeled "unfit" of little worth.
Indignant words rose to my lips, but were never set
free,
For every face showed stunned surprise, no one
expected ME.

FROM THE POEM, *SURPRISE*

Forgiveness does not change the past,
but it does enlarge the future.

PAUL BOESE

When you hold resentment toward another, you are
bound to that person by an emotional link that is
stronger than steel. Forgiveness is the only way to
dissolve that link and get free.

CATHERINE PONDER

FREEDOM

Freedom is not the right to do what we want, but what we ought. Let us have faith that right makes might, and in that faith, let us, to the end, dare to do our duty as we understand it.

ABRAHAM LINCOLN

Freedom is nothing else but a chance to be better.

ALBERT CAMUS

Liberty will not descend to a people; a people must raise themselves to liberty; it is a blessing that must be earned before it can be enjoyed.

CHARLES CALEB COLTON

Whenever a separation is made between liberty and justice, neither is safe.

EDMUND BURKE

So far as a person thinks, they are free.

RALPH WALDO EMERSON

A country cannot subsist without liberty nor liberty without virtue.

JEAN JACQUES ROUSSEAU

Freedom is never voluntarily given by the oppressor; it must be demanded by the oppressed.

MARTIN LUTHER KING, JR.

If a nation values anything more than freedom, it will lose its freedom; and the irony of it is that if it is comfort or money that it values more, it will lose that, too.

SOMERSET MAUGHAM

The last of the human freedoms is the ability to choose one's response to any given situation.
VICTOR FRANKL - A PRISONER OF WAR HELD BY THE NAZIS

True individual freedom cannot exist without economic security and independence. People who are hungry and out of a job are the stuff of which dictatorships are made.
FRANKLIN D. ROOSEVELT

GRATITUDE & THANKFULNESS

The more we express our gratitude to God for our blessings, the more he will bring to our minds other blessings. The more we are aware of to be grateful for, the happier we become.
EZRA TAFT BENSON

We can only be said to be alive in those moments when our hearts are conscious of our treasures.
THORNTON WILDER

Let the thankful heart sweep through the day and, as the magnet finds iron, so it will find in every hour, some heavenly blessings.
HENRY WARD BEECHER

How wonderful it would be if we could help our children and grandchildren to learn thanksgiving at an early age. Thanksgiving opens doors. It changes a child's personality. A child is resentful, negative or thankful. Thankful children want to give, they radiate happiness, they draw people.
SIR JOHN TEMPLETON

If you have nothing to be grateful for, check your pulse.
UNKNOWN

When we were children we were grateful for those who filled our stockings at Christmas time. Why are we not then grateful to God for filling our stockings with legs?
G. K. CHESTERTON

Would you know who is the greatest saint in the world: it is not he who prays most or fasts most. It is not he who gives the most alms or is most eminent for temperance, chastity or justice; but it is he who is always thankful to God, who wills everything that God wills, who receives everything as an instance of God's goodness and has a heart always ready to praise God for it.
WILLIAM LAW

You're not going to make me have a bad day. If there's oxygen on earth and I'm breathing, it's going to be a good day.
COTTON FITZSIMMONS

Silent gratitude isn't much good to anyone.
GLADYS BROWYN STERN

We would all like a reputation for generosity, and we'd all like to buy it cheap.
MIGNON MCLAUGHLIN

GROWTH

[The Jonah Complex is]... the evasion of one's own growth, the setting of low levels of aspiration, the fear of doing what one is capable of doing, voluntary self-crippling, pseudo-stupidity, mock humility."

ABRAHAM MASLOW - *DESCRIBING THE JONAH COMPLEX*

Oh my friend, it's not what they take away from you that counts. It's what you do with what you have left.

HUBERT HUMPHREY

With each passage of human growth, we must shed a protective structure (like a hardy crustacean). We are left exposed and vulnerable — but also yeasty and embryonic again, capable of stretching in ways we hadn't known before.

GAIL SHEEHY

One can have no smaller or greater mastery
than mastery of oneself.

LEONARDO DA VINCI

As a searching investigator of the integrity of your own conduct, submit your life to a daily examination. Consider carefully what progress you have made or what ground you have lost. Strive to know yourself. Place all your faults before your eyes. Come face to face with yourself.

SAINT BERNARD

So what if you make mistakes?

POPE FRANCIS

If I were to wish for anything... it would be for the passionate sense of what can be, for the eye which, ever young and ardent, sees the possible.

SOREN KIERKEGAARD

Many people's tombstones should read, "Died at 30. Buried at 60."

NICHOLAS MURRAY BUTLER

For the first half of your life, people tell you what you should do; for the second half, they tell you what you should have done.

RICHARD NEEDHAM

We should every night call ourselves to an account. What infirmity have I mastered today? What passions opposed? What temptation resisted? What virtue acquired? Our vices will abort themselves if they be brought every day to the shrift.

SENECA, *ROMAN PHILOSOPHER*

There is no clock, no matter how good it may be, that doesn't need resetting and rewinding twice a day, once in the morning and once in the evening. In addition, at least once a year it must be taken apart to remove the dirt clogging it, straighten out its bent parts, and repair those worn out. In like manner, every morning and evening a man who really takes care of his heart must rewind it for God's service.

ST. FRANCIS DE SALES

Start by doing what is necessary, then what is possible, and suddenly you are doing the impossible.

ST. FRANCIS OF ASSISI

Anyone who stops learning is old,
whether this happens at twenty or at eighty.
HENRY FORD

HEALING

Tears have a wisdom of their own. They are the natural bleeding of an emotional wound, carrying the poison out of the system. Here lies the road to recovery.
F. ALEXANDER MAGOUN

All I know from my experience is that the more loss we feel, the more grateful we should be for whatever it was we had to lose. It means that we had something worth grieving for. The ones I'm feeling sorry for are the ones that go through life without knowing what grief is.
FRANK O'CONNOR

When one has not had a good father, one must create one.
FRIEDRICH NIETZCHE

Grief is itself a medicine.
WILLIAM COWPER

HOLINESS

A man does not have to be an angel to be a saint.
ALBERT SCHWEITZER

They are not all saints who use holy water.
ENGLISH PROVERB

Holiness is not something that comes from doing good; we do good because we are holy. Holiness is not something we acquire by avoiding evil: we avoid evil because we are holy. Holiness is not something that follows from prayer: we pray because we are holy. Holiness is not the result of kindness: we are kind because we are holy. Holiness is not something that blossoms when we are courageous: we are courageous because we are holy. Holiness is not the result of character building: we build character because we are holy. Holiness is not a gift we obtain after a lifetime of service; we give service because we are holy.

FR. JOHN CATOIR

Sanctity is not a matter of being less human, but more human than other men. This implies a greater capacity for concern, for suffering, for understanding, for sympathy, and also for humor, for joy, for appreciation of the good and beautiful things of life.

THOMAS MERTON - ON "SANCTITY"

HOPE & PERSEVERANCE

Anyone can give up; it's the easiest thing in the world to do. But to hold it together when everyone else would understand if you fell apart — that's true strength.

ANONYMOUS

It's often the last key on the ring which opens the door.

ANONYMOUS

Impossible things just take a little longer.

PHILO T. FARNSWORTH

What you spend years building, someone could destroy overnight: build anyway! If you find serenity and happiness, they may be jealous: be happy anyway! The good you do today, people will often forget tomorrow: do good anyway! Give the world the best you have, and it may never be enough: give the world the best you've got anyway! You see, in the final analysis, it is between you and God – it was never between you and them anyway!

MOTHER TERESA

Adversity has the effect of eliciting talents which,
in prosperous circumstances, would have lain dormant.

HORACE

Through all the tumult and the strife,
I hear the music ringing.
It sounds and echoes in my soul;
how can I keep from singing?
What though the tempest 'round me roar,
I hear the truth it liveth.
What though the darkness round me close,
songs in the night it giveth.

QUAKER HYMN - *HOW CAN I KEEP FROM SINGING*

Nobody grows old merely by living a number of years. We grow old by deserting our ideals. Age may wrinkle the skin, but to give up enthusiasm wrinkles the soul.

SAMUEL ULLMAN

Every parent is at some time the father of the unreturned prodigal, with nothing to do but keep his house open to hope.

JOHN CIARDI

Do not look forward in fear; rather look forward with full hope. God, whose very own you are, will lead you safely through all things, and when you cannot stand it any longer, he will carry you in his arms. Do not fear what may happen tomorrow; the same good God who cares for you today will take care of you then and every day of your life. He will either shield you from suffering or will give you the unfailing strength to bear it. Be at peace, and put aside all your anxious thoughts and imaginations.

ST. FRANCIS DE SALES

That which doesn't kill you, makes you stronger.

FRIEDRICH NIETZSCHE

HUMOR

An archeologist is the best husband a woman can have. The older she gets the more interested he is in her.

AGATHA CHRISTIE

First you forget names, then you forget faces.
Next you forget to pull your zipper up and finally,
you forget to pull it down.

GEORGE BURNS

I can take reality in small doses,
but as a way of life I find it much too confining.

LILY TOMLIN AS HER CHARACTER, "TRUDY"

Always tell the truth.
That way, you don't have to remember what you said.

MARK TWAIN

Be nice to your children,
for they will choose your rest home."
PHYLLIS DILLER

Housework can't kill you, but why take the chance?
PHYLLIS DILLER

It is useless to hold a person to anything he says
while he's in love, drunk or running for office.
SHIRLEY MACLAINE

God is a comedian, playing to an audience
too afraid to laugh.
VOLTAIRE

The years between 50 and 70 are the hardest. You are
always being asked to do more, and you are not yet
decrepit enough to turn them down.
T. S. ELIOT

Live in such a way that you would not be ashamed
to sell your parrot to the town gossip.
WILL ROGERS

HYPOCRISY

A hypocrite is a man who murders both his parents and then
pleads for mercy on the grounds that he is an orphan.
ABRAHAM LINCOLN

The true hypocrite is the one who ceases to perceive
his deception, the one who lies with sincerity.
ANDRE GIDE

Moral indignation is jealousy with a halo.
H. G. WELLS

A great deal of what passes for current Christianity
consists in denouncing other people's vices and faults.
HENRY H. JAMES

Loud indignation against vice often stands for
virtue in the eyes of bigots.
J. PETIT-SENN

Most of us are aware of and pretend to detest the
barefaced instances of hypocrisy by which men deceive others, but few of us are on our guard or see
that more fatal hypocrisy by which we deceive and
over-reach our own hearts.
LAURENCE STERN

One should examine oneself for a very long time
before thinking of condemning others.
MOLIERE

LIFE

One can remain alive long past the usual date of dis-
integration if one is unafraid of change, insatiable in
intellectual curiosity, interested in big things, and
happy in a small way.
EDITH WHARTON

Be a force of nature instead of a feverish, selfish little clod of ailments and grievances, complaining that
the world will not devote itself to making you happy.
GEORGE BERNARD SHAW

For peace of mind, resign as general manager of the universe.
ANONYMOUS

I have studied many times the marble which was chiseled for me — a boat with a furled sail at rest in the harbor. In truth it pictures not my destination but my life. For love was offered me, and I shrank from its disillusionment; sorrow knocked at my door, but I was afraid; ambition called to me, but I dreaded the chances. Yet all the while I hungered for meaning in my life. And now I know I must lift the sail and catch the winds of destiny wherever they drive the boat. To put meaning in one's life may end in madness, but life without meaning is the torture of restlessness and vague desire — it is a boat longing for the sea and yet afraid.

EDGAR LEE MASTERS IN *GEORGE GRAY*

The indispensable first step to getting the things you want out of life is this: Decide what you want.

BEN STEIN

He not busy being born is busy dying.

BOB DYLAN

This is the true joy in life, the being used for a purpose recognized by yourself as a mighty one; the being thoroughly worn out before you are thrown on the scrap heap.

GEORGE BERNARD SHAW

Our culture has become most sophisticated in the avoidance of pain, not only our physical pain but our mental and emotional pain as well... We have become so used to this state of anesthesia that we panic when there is nothing or nobody to distract us.

HENRI NOUWEN

I have heard it said that heroism can be redefined for our age as the ability to tolerate paradox, to embrace seemingly opposing forces without rejecting one or the other just for the sheer relief of it, and to understand that life is the game played between two paradoxical goalposts: winning is good and so is losing; freedom is good and so is authority; having and giving; action and passivity; sex and celibacy; income and outgo; courage and fear. Both are true. They may sit on opposite sides of the table, but underneath it their legs are entwined.

GREGG LEVOY IN *CALLINGS*

Keep your mind on the things you want and
off the things you don't want.
HANNAH WHITHALL SMITH

Most men lead lives of quiet desperation and
go to their graves with the song still in them.
HENRY DAVID THOREAU

The saddest summary of life contains three descriptions:
could have, might have and should have!
LOUIS E. BOONE

The change in emphasis in our relationships and our society from "me" to "we" will not erode individual rights, ability, achievement, freedom of expression or ownership in any way. Nor will it require that we relinquish our hard-earned cash or possessions, repudiate our economic system or overturn our democratic way of life. The only thing we will give up is the need to strive for individual achievement at another's expense.

LYNNE TAGGART

The most important thing a father can do for
his children is to love their mother.
HENRY WARD BEECHER

By running away from our loneliness and by trying
to distract ourselves with people and special experiences, we are in danger of becoming unhappy people
suffering from many unsatisfied cravings and tor-
tured by desires and expectations that never can be
fulfilled.
HENRI NOUWEN

We ask ourselves, who am I to be brilliant, gorgeous,
talented and fabulous? You are a child of God. Your
playing small doesn't serve the world. There is nothing enlightened about shrinking so that other people
won't feel insecure around us. We were born to make
manifest the glory of God that is within us.
MARIANNE WILLIAMSON

Opportunity is missed by most because it is
dressed in overalls and looks like work.
THOMAS A. EDISON

The first half of life consists of the capacity to
enjoy without the chance; the last half consists
of the chance without the capacity.
MARK TWAIN

Death is not the greatest loss in life.
The greatest loss is what dies within us while we live.
NORMAN COUSINS

One must attend carefully to everything. If you apply
yourself carefully to what you do, great springs of
strength and truth are realized in you.
THOMAS MERTON

Besides the noble art of getting things done, there is the nobler art of leaving things undone. The wisdom of life consists in the elimination of nonessentials.
LIN YUTANG

LOVE & KINDNESS

Constant kindness can accomplish much. As the sun makes ice melt, kindness causes misunderstanding, mistrust and hostility to evaporate.
ALBERT SCHWEITZER

Correction does much, but encouragement does more.
JOHANN WOLFGANG GOETHE

It's the Holy Spirit's job to convict,
God's job to judge and my job to love.
BILLY GRAHAM

I'd rather have sticks and stones and broken bones than the words you say to me, cause I know bruises heal and cuts will seal but your words beat the life from me.
DAVE BARNES IN HIS SONG, *STICKS AND STONES*

Kindness has converted more sinners
than zeal, eloquence or learning.
F. W. FABER

One word or a pleasing smile is often enough to raise up a saddened and wounded soul.
SAINT TERESA OF LISIEUX

The biggest human temptation is to settle for too little.
THOMAS MERTON

Blessed is the servant who loves his brother as much when he is sick and useless as when he is well and can be of service to him, and blessed is he who loves his brother as well when he is afar off as when he is by his side and who would say nothing behind his back he might not, in love, say before his face.

ST. FRANCIS OF ASSISI

It is much easier to become a father than be one.

KENT NERBURN

Right from the moment of our birth, we are under the care and kindness of our parents, and then later on in our life when we are oppressed by sickness and become old, we are again dependent on the kindness of others. Since at the beginning and the end of our lives we are so dependent on others' kindness, how can it be in the middle that we would neglect kindness toward others?

DALAI LAMA

REST, RENEWAL & PEACE

There is no need to go to India or anywhere else to find peace. You will find that deep place of silence right in your room, your garden or even your bathtub.

ELIZABETH KUBLER-ROSS

If a man insisted always on being serious, and never allowed himself a bit of fun and relaxation, he would go mad or become unstable without knowing it.

HERODOTUS

Take rest; a field that has rested gives a bountiful crop.
OVID

TRUTH

The truth is often a terrible weapon of aggression.
It is possible to lie, and even murder, with the truth.
ALFRED ADLER

Believe those who are seeking the truth;
doubt those who find it.
ANDRE GIDE

When a well-packaged web of lies has been sold gradually to the masses over generations, the truth will seem utterly preposterous and its speaker a raving lunatic.
DRESDEN JAMES

During times of universal deceit,
telling the truth becomes a revolutionary act.
GEORGE ORWELL

One truth out of context can prove very dangerous.
GREGORY PHILLIPS

The truth will set you free,
but first it will make you miserable.
JAMES A. GARFIELD

The enemy of the truth is very often not the lie — deliberate, contrived and dishonest, but the myth — persistent, persuasive and unrealistic.
JOHN F. KENNEDY

I believe that unarmed truth and unconditional love
will have the final word in reality. This is why right,
temporarily defeated, is stronger than evil triumphant.

MARTIN LUTHER KING, JR.

Nothing in all the world is more dangerous
than sincere ignorance and conscious stupidity.

MARTIN LUTHER KING, JR.

The truth is 'hate speech' only to those
who have something to hide.

MICHAEL RIVERO

It's discouraging to think how many people are shocked
by honesty and how few by deceit.

NOEL COWARD

A thing is not necessarily true because a man dies for it.

OSCAR WILDE

The truth is rarely pure and never simple.

OSCAR WILDE

Sometimes the majority only means that
all the fools are on the same side.

UNKNOWN

From the cowardice that shrinks from new truth;
from laziness that is content with half-truths;
from the arrogance that thinks it knows all truth —
O God of Truth deliver us!

UNKNOWN

If a thousand old beliefs were ruined in our march to truth
we must still march on.

TOM WAITS

The news and the truth are not the same thing.
WALTER LIPPMANN

Truth often suffers more by the heat of its defenders than the arguments of its opposers.
WILLIAM PENN

WORK

I long to accomplish great and noble tasks, but it is my chief duty to accomplish humble tasks as though they were great and noble. The world is moved along not only by the mighty shoves of its heroes, but also by the aggregate of the tiny pushes of each honest worker.
HELEN KELLER

Work while you have the light. You are responsible for the talent that has been entrusted to you.
HENRI F. AMIEL

The secret of joy in work is contained in one word – excellence. To know how to do something well is to enjoy it.
PEARL BUCK

Made in the USA
San Bernardino, CA
19 November 2013